OSPREY
PUBLISHING

Greek Hoplite 480–323 BC

Nicholas Sekunda • Illustrated by Adam Hook

First published in Great Britain in 2000 by Osprey Publishing, Elms Court,
Chapel Way, Botley, Oxford OX2 9LP, United Kingdom.
Email: info@ospreypublishing.com

CIP Data for this publication is available from the British Library

ISBN 1 85532 867 4

Editor: Nikolai Bogdanovic
Design: Alan Hamp
Originated by Valhaven, Isleworth, UK
Printed in China through World Print Ltd.

Index by Alan Rutter

FOR A CATALOGUE OF ALL BOOKS PUBLISHED BY
OSPREY MILITARY AND AVIATION PLEASE CONTACT:

The Marketing Manager, Osprey Direct UK, PO Box 140,
Wellingborough, Northants, NN8 2FA, United Kingdom.
Email: info@ospreydirect.co.uk

The Marketing Manager, Osprey Direct USA,
c/o MBI Publishing, PO Box 1,
729 Prospect Avenue, Osceola, WI 54020, USA.
Email: info@ospreydirectusa.com

www.ospreypublishing.com

Artist's Note

Readers may care to note that the original paintings from which the
colour plates in this book were prepared are available for private
sale. All reproduction copyright whatsoever is retained by the
Publishers. All enquiries should be addressed to:

Scorpio Gallery, PO Box 475, Hailsham, Sussex, UK.

The Publishers regret that they can enter into no correspondence
upon this matter.

Acknowledgements

I would like to thank my friend Richard Brzezinski for his help in
producing a much better text than would otherwise have been
the case. I would also like to thank Lee Johnson and Nikolai
Bogdanovic at Osprey for their help and patience.

GREEK HOPLITE 480–323 BC

INTRODUCTION

WAR IS NOT the first thing that comes to mind when one thinks of ancient Greece. Sculpture, philosophy, drama are all facets of human endeavour for which Greece is justly famous. Yet for the ancient Greeks war was a far more immediate concern, and pervaded all spheres of political, cultural and intellectual endeavour. Warfare was the subject of most of the surviving Greek tragedies and comedies; warriors and warfare are the most common subjects of Greek sculptures and vases, while much of Classical Greek philosophy was concerned with the role of the hoplite: the citizen-soldier.

Greece was divided into hundreds of city-states (*poleis*, singular *polis*), and armed conflict between them was common. Plato (*Laws* 626 A) argued that peace is but a word, and that every state was, by nature, engaged in a permanent undeclared war with every other state. War also pervaded Greek religion. Unlike modern faiths it did not have a 'holy book' of revelatory wisdom: the nearest equivalent was the *Iliad*, set against a background of Greeks at war.

The Greek word for 'weapon' is *hoplon*, and so a hoplite was literally a 'man at arms' (see Lazenby & Whitehead, *Classical Quarterly* 46 (1996) 27–33). Hoplites, heavily armoured Greek infantrymen, dominated Greek warfare for some four centuries. They fought in a close formation called a phalanx, which in Greek has a general meaning of 'battle-formation', but which modern authorities frequently apply exclusively to the heavy infantry formation.

This book is aimed at the general reader who may well be familiar with the works of Herodotus or Thucydides, and who may wish to know a little more about the hoplite: his equipment, training and life on campaign, and also how an infantry battle was fought in ancient Greece.

As far as we can tell, the hoplite rose to the position

Although the hero Astyochos, perhaps unrealistically, is depicted naked, there are several interesting features on this painting of c.420. He holds his long spear underarm and crouches low behind his shield swung in front of the body, face hidden behind the rim and shoulder pressed into the hollow of the shield. Detail of a battle between Greeks and Amazons by Aison on a squat lekythos. (Museo Nazionale, Naples, inv. RC239; © Hirmer Fotoarchiv-Nr. 57i.0539)

of 'queen of the battlefield' during the early 7th century BC. His authority in the field was first seriously challenged by the advance of the Persian empire to the Aegean coast in 546, which brought about dramatic changes in hoplite tactics. This book concentrates on the hoplite during the 'Classical period', which is generally considered as running from the battle of Salamis in 480 to the death of Alexander the Great in 323. During this period the hoplite had already lost his monopoly of the battlefield, and increasing use was being made of cavalry and light infantry.

No description of a hoplite battle before the Classical period has survived. The first actions described in any detail are those of the Persian Wars, which, it should be remembered, were not fought against other hoplites. Then there is a long gap before the Peloponnesian War (431–404) and Thucydides' description of the few major battles of that conflict.

Of supreme value are the works of Xenophon, who in 401 took part in the expedition of 10,000 Greek mercenaries into Asia Minor, hired by Cyrus the Younger to seize the Persian throne. Xenophon joined the expedition as a gentleman volunteer, aged under 30, and because of his character and ability, was elected commander by the mercenaries themselves. As well as an epic account of the expedition, he penned works on history, economics and a host of other subjects. He describes military incidents with deep understanding, and it is Xenophon, more than any other single Greek author, who allows us to really understand the mechanics of hoplite warfare.

Victor Davis Hanson, *The Western Way of War. Infantry Battle in Classical Greece* (1989), is recommended to those who wish to read further into the subject. A work edited by Hanson, *Hoplites: The Classical Greek Battle Experience* (1991), also contains much useful material. J. K. Anderson, *Military Theory & Practice in the Age of Xenophon* (1970), is recommended for its treatment of the new hoplite tactics introduced during the Classical period. The standard handbook on hoplite equipment remains A. M. Snodgrass, *Arms and Armour of the Greeks* (1967). So that the interested reader can consult Xenophon and the other primary sources, I have included source references, mainly following the standard abbreviations used, for example, in the *Oxford Classical Dictionary*. All dates are BC unless otherwise stated.

RIGHT **This stele, erected at Megara during the Peloponnesian War, is inscribed on the front and sides with a list of the city's dead. The list is ordered by the city-state's three Dorian tribes: the Dymanes, Hylleis and Pamphyloi. The last two names appear as sub-headings. (Photo and drawing by Kritzas in *Philia ... Mylonas* 3 (1989) p.168, p.44)**

THE CITIZEN SOLDIER

Hoplites served in the armies of kings and tyrants, but the hoplite was, in essence, a citizen-soldier. It was the duty of the citizen in all free Greek states to perform military service. Any assembly of citizens was by definition a gathering of warriors past and present. Fundamentally every Greek citizen was a hoplite.

Organisation

The political and military organisation of the Greek city-states were intimately connected. The citizen-hoplites were organised into 'tribes' unrelated by blood. Tribes are briefly mentioned in Homer's *Iliad* but these passages are obviously late insertions dating to the end of the

8th century BC when Homer's text reached its final form. The tribe replaced the warrior band of the Greek Dark Ages.

Tribes were organised by dividing the state's hoplite population into politico-military groupings of equal size. These groupings inevitably began to vary in size as a result of natural processes, births, deaths, and losses in battle. Over time it would be necessary to replace the existing tribal structure with a new one, often based on a different territorial basis.

Tribes were originally sub-divided into *phratries*, or 'brotherhoods'. The military functions of the phratry eventually died out as a result of successive tribal reforms. Because phratries were founded under a common oath of its unrelated members to stick together in battle, and were placed under the protection of a deity, it would have been sacrilege to dissolve such a body. Therefore they survive as 'fossil' institutions with purely religious and social functions in many Greek states. The organisations which replaced phratries as the sub-divisions of the tribe were normally given titles with kin or numerical associations, like the *genos* 'family' or the *triakas* 'thirty'. These too would have to be replaced in time, but might survive as 'fossil' social and religious institutions.

Training

The method by which a male child was registered into the citizen body, and therefore for military service, varied from state to state. The Athenian system is best understood. Each city-state had its own calendar, but in general the year began at the end of the summer. In most states military training began for all boys aged 18 at the beginning of the civic year. Lists of citizens would be maintained at the lowest level of politico-military organisation within the tribe, and upon 'coming of age' the claims of the boy to citizenship would be checked against these lists and the names of new members entered upon them.

The new soldier-citizens would now be gathered together and would swear a common oath. The oath sworn by the young Athenians in the Temple of Aglauros has been preserved:

I shall not dishonour these sacred arms, nor leave the man stationed beside me in the line. I will defend both the sacred and secular places and not hand over the fatherland smaller, but greater and mightier as far as I and all are able, and I shall listen to those in power at the time and the laws which have been drawn up and those that will be, and if anyone will abolish them I shall

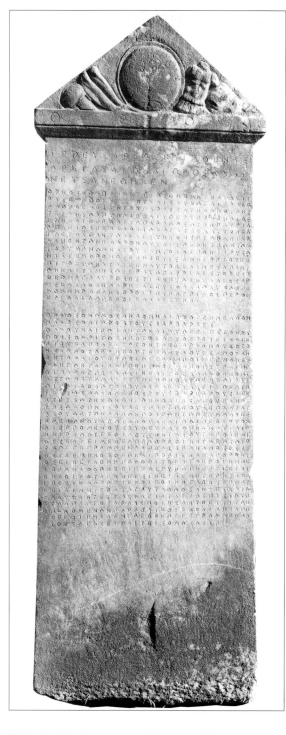

Stele, found in the sanctuary of the war god Ares at Acharnae in AD 1932, now in the French School at Athens. It records the Athenian ephebic oath and the oath taken by the Greeks before the battle of Plataea fought in 479 against the Persians. The defensive armour of a hoplite is shown in the tympanum. The object to the right of the cuirass is probably a folded cloak. (© French School at Athens No.12.300)

not give way to them as far as I and all are able, and I will honour the ancestral cults. My witnesses are the gods Aglauros, Hestia, Enyo, Enyalios, Ares and Athena Areia, Zeus, Thallo, Auxo, Hegemone, Herakles, the boundaries of the fatherland, and her wheat, barley, vines, olive and fig trees.

These young men were now called *epheboi* (ephebes or 'youths'), and for the next two years they underwent a programme of physical and military training, the 'ephebate'. Some form of ephebate is attested in most Greek states, but practice varied greatly. In the Archaic period ephebic training may have been rudimentary and haphazard, but it became increasingly organised and sophisticated with time. Furthermore far greater funds were available to provide organised training in the larger and richer city-states.

In Athens the first year of ephebic training was taken up with a cycle of athletic contests, mainly running races, organised by tribe. The most important of these were torch-races, either individual or team events, connected with religious festivals. The races at some festivals were individual in which all ephebes competed, while the races at others were team events, the torch being passed by relay. Such races are also attested in a multitude of other Greek states, as is the office of *gymnasiarchos*. The gymnasiarch was a wealthy citizen elected by his fellow-tribesmen to organise the training of the ephebes to ensure the victory of the tribe team in the races. He paid for materials and perhaps food to allow the ephebes to devote more of their time to training. The principal raw material required was olive oil: after taking exercise athletes rubbed this oil into the skin and scraped themselves clean with a bronze tool called a strigil.

The 'Pyrrhic' dance in armour (named after its supposed inventor Purrhikhos) was another popular element in ephebic training. It originated in Archaic times as a means of training young warriors in the moves required to avoid enemy blows and to deliver their own. Individual and team contests were organised for the armoured dance, usually at religious festivals.

Another organised activity of military character was the hoplite race *(hoplitodromos)*, introduced at Olympia in 520 and Delphi in 498. It appeared after Greek armies first came into contact with Persian archery. The race was originally run over a distance of 400 metres – enough to take the hoplite through the 'beaten zone' of enemy archery and up to the Persian line. The hoplite race accustomed the ephebe to carrying the shield and developed general strength.

The shields shown being used in hoplite races on Attic vases frequently have identical shield devices. This suggests that publicly owned sets of shields of equal weight were specially commissioned for the hoplite race. Surviving inventories of arsenals and temple magazines mention sets of shields or 'light shields' (*aspidiskoi*), presumably for use in the hoplite race. The shields were normally decorated with the symbols of the god in whose temple the shields were stored and in whose honour and at whose festival the hoplite race was run. A typical example was the sun or swastika symbol for Apollo. Other sets of shields are marked with the initials 'A' or 'ATHE' for the goddess Athena.

A hoplite, with helmet, spear and shield, dances the Pyrrhic dance to the tune of a flute. Scene from the tondo of a kylix cup painted about 490 by the Eucharides Painter. (M. et P. Chuzeville, Louvre, Paris, inv. G136)

The prizes awarded in all these competitions were symbolic in value rather than financial. The typical prize was an olive wreath, which frequently appears on funerary or commemorative monuments as a symbol of victory in the competitions achieved by the gymnasiarch of the tribe.

We hear that in many states ephebes were adopted by older young men who had completed their military training, but who were still regularly training in the gymnasia. The system might be compared to the 'buddy-buddy' system worked by many modern armies, where a young soldier is adopted by an experienced one, who teaches him the tricks of the trade, shares his trench, etc. In ancient Greek these pairs are called 'lovers' which has given rise to much confusion among modern scholars. It is clear that the word is not to be taken in its carnal sense, and sexual contact between these pairs of 'lovers' was frowned upon. For example Xenophon (*Lak. Pol.* 2. 13) states that in Sparta sexual relations between 'lovers' was banned.

Nevertheless sexual contact between these pairs of young men did take place. Plato (*Laws* 636 B) speaks of how the gymnasia corrupt the natural sexual desires which are common to men and beasts, and in the Athenian comedies the gymnasia are characterised, needless to say with considerable comic exaggeration, as places frequented by homosexuals. Likewise Xenophon (*Symp.* 8. 31–7), in the course of a discussion of the pros and cons of spiritual as opposed to carnal 'love' among young men,

Ephebic hoplites running the *hoplitodromos*. The ephebe on the right is instructing the one in the centre how to place his hand on the start-line in the 'get ready' position. Note the near identical shield devices showing a hoplite runner. From a scene on a kylix cup painted around the 480s by the Antiphon Painter. (Antikensammlung, Staatliche Museen zu Berlin – Preussischer Kulturbesitz, inv. F2307)

singles out Thebes and Elis as hot-beds of these practices. It is impossible to state how widespread homosexuality was in ancient Greece: probably no more so than in modern Greece.

The second year of ephebic training was generally more intensive and military in character. In many states the ephebes lived together, away from home, in barracks. They provided permanent garrisons for the city-state's key defensive points: the fortified citadel (*acropolis*) of the city and the forts and watch-towers along the border, guarding against surprise attacks by neighbouring states. In some states ephebes patrolled the borders and countryside, and were called *peripoloi*, 'patrollers' or literally 'those who travel about'. These long periods of absence in the countryside evolved into ritual periods of seclusion marking the end of childhood and the entry into manhood.

The hoplite was not a warrior who fought individually. He was a component of the phalanx, a line of hoplites drawn up in ranks who stabbed with their spears from behind a wall of shields. According to King Damaratus, Spartan soldiers could lose their helmet or breastplate with impunity, but would be disgraced if they threw away their shield: 'For they wear the former for their own sakes, but carry shields for the whole line' (Plut., *Mor.* 220 a). It was imperative that the hoplite kept his place calmly in the line; once disordered the shield wall would be easily broken.

Xenophon (*Mem.* 3.1.8) compared the arrangement of the hoplite line to the construction of a house. The best materials which do not crumble away, stones and tiles, are used for the roof and foundations, while mud bricks and timbers are 'fillers' placed in the middle. The best men should be placed at the front and rear of the line, the worst in the centre. In that way the poorer men will be drawn forward by the bravery of the front rank and pushed forward by the pressure of those to the rear. When speaking of the cavalry file Xenophon (*Cavalry Commander* 2.2–4) recommends that the commander should appoint young men in the prime of life and ambitious to win fame as file-leaders, and older and more sensible men as file-closers. In that way the file would have the most cutting power, like a blade 'with its edge keen and its back sturdy'.

The file-leaders should be allowed to choose the second man in the file, the second the third, and so on, so that all would have confidence in the man behind him. In the Lakedaimonian army the younger age-classes were stationed in the front ranks and the older ones in the rear. (e.g. Xen., *Hell.* 4.6.10). The file did not have a standard number of ranks, this varied over time. At the beginning of the Classical period there is some indication that decimal systems were preferred. Later, a file of 16 men, giving a half-file of eight, seems to have become standard (Xen., *Hell.* 4.2.18).

Consequently ephebic training concentrated on group tactics. There was far less stress on individual weapon skills, such as sword fencing. Private instructors, called *hoplomachoi*, 'fighters in arms', gave extra tuition in the art of close fighting, for a fee.

In some states the ephebate ended with a formal parade of the new warriors in the theatre. In late 4th century BC Athens this took place at the end of the first year's training, but it had perhaps earlier taken place at the end of the final year. The ephebes paraded in armour and displayed the manoeuvres they had learned.

EQUIPMENT

Weapons only started to be issued by the state towards the end of the Classical period, earlier on it was the duty of the citizen-hoplite to supply his own. Hoplite equipment was expensive. A late 6th century BC Athenian decree required settlers on Salamis to provide themselves with a panoply to the value of 30 drachmas (Jackson, in *Hoplites* p.229), a month's pay for an artisan in Classical Athens. Such was the cost of weapons that they were usually handed down from father to son (Plut., *Mor.* 241 F 17).

Achilles and Memnon fight in this scene from a kylix cup of about 500. Memnon's spear has passed through and stuck fast in Achilles' shield, failing to wound the hero. Memnon is now defenceless, allowing Achilles to strike the death blow with an overarm thrust. (American School of Classical Studies at Athens: Agora Excavations, inv. P24113)

The ancient Greek 'weapons industry' was concentrated in the larger cities. Smaller cities usually imported their weapons. Pericles persuaded the foreigner Kephalos, the father of the Athenian orator Lysias (12.19, 14.6), to establish a shield factory in Athens. It employed 120 slaves, the largest workforce attested for any factory in the ancient city.

The most important item of hoplite equipment was the shield (*aspis*). Protective quality was sacrificed for lightness and overall cover. Weighing about 6.2kg (13.5 pounds), the hoplite shield was capable of turning a spear- or sword-thrust, but was not proof against arrows or javelins. Many vase paintings show pierced hoplite shields. The Spartan general Brasidas was wounded when his shield 'turned traitor' (Plut., *Mor.* 219 C). Xenophon (*An.* 4.1.18) describes how Leonymos the Lakonian died when a spear went through his shield. The hoplite valued his mobility more than complete protection.

When the ancients or moderns refer to the hoplite shield as bronze, they are referring to the extremely thin (less than half a millimetre thick) bronze covering. The main component of the shield was its wooden base. In the Archaic period only the rim of the shield was reinforced with bronze, though the blazon on the front might also be made in bronze. In Archaic vase-painting the shield's surface was usually rendered in black but the bronze rim and blazon in red. Around 500 the Greeks developed the technology to cover the entire outer surface of the shield with a thin plate of stressed bronze. Blazons were now painted directly onto the shield's bronze surface. The conventions of vase-painting changed: shield-rim and surface alike were now shown in red and blazons in black. When shown in profile the Classical shield also had a more deeply curving shape than its Archaic counterpart. The rim

The outer covering of the hoplite shield was an extremely thin sheet of bronze. This shield, some 84–87cm in diameter, including a 5–5.5cm rim, emerged from the ground during German excavations at Olympia. It was dedicated by the city of Zankle (modern Messina in Sicily) in the 490s as spoil taken from the hoplites of Rhegion in southern Italy. (German Archaeological Institute, Athens Neg. Ol. 1963)

was normally embossed with a guilloche pattern. The rim provided rigidity to the bowl of the shield, preventing it from buckling easily in battle. It was one of the most distinctive features of the hoplite shield, as the ancients themselves recognised when they compared it with other Greek shields.

The helmet too was not expected to ward off all blows: strength was sacrificed for lightness and reasonable all-over protection. Hoplites used several varieties of close-helmet which must have seriously restricted hearing and vision. The inside was sometimes lined with fabric, but lacked the strap suspension system found in modern helmets. Blows to the head must have frequently resulted in injury. Hoplites are normally shown wearing nothing under the helmet, though occasional representations show that a cloth head-band, or caps of various styles, were often worn for comfort. Homer (*Il.* 10.258) terms the leather cap worn in battle *kataityx*, but we do not know if this term was used later for 'cap-comforters' of this type.

The brightly dyed horsehair crests attached to Greek helmets were mainly designed to make the hoplite appear taller and more imposing (Jackson in *Hoplites* 235). In the later Classical period, when the concept of uniform began to develop, the crest also served as a badge of rank. The helmet of the general Lamachus (Aristophanes, *Acharn.* 1103, 9), was decorated with three crests and two plumes.

The hoplite of the early 5th century BC used two types of cuirass: the muscle cuirass and the composite cuirass. The muscle cuirass is so-called because the bronze breast- and back-plates were modelled to imitate the musculature of the torso. It developed out of the Archaic 'bell-cuirass', named after the flange which flared outwards below the waist like the mouth of a bell. This flange disappears in the Classical period and the muscle-cuirass curves down to cover the groin.

The composite cuirass is so-called because it was constructed from composite materials, normally scales or plates made of iron or bronze, often covered with leather or linen to prevent rusting. Temple dedications of such cuirasses all disintegrated long ago. The first intact example was discovered in 1977 in the tomb of Philip II of Macedon. References to linen or leather armour perhaps refer to composite cuirasses covered with these materials, though armour made exclusively from layers of hardened leather or linen may also have been used. Armour made from linen stiffened by soaking in vinegar and salt was used in the Byzantine period.

The groin was protected by a double layer of groin-flaps, called *pteruges* or 'wings' in Greek, the second layer covering the gaps in the first. They were made of stiffened leather rather than of metal. Most have a coloured border and a fringe at the lower end. Pteruges were an integral part of the design of the cuirass, and were permanently attached to its bottom edge.

An early Corinthian helmet, manufactured in two halves, which shows extensive battle-damage and repair. Note the cracks above each eye-hole and the partially preserved patch above the left eye. The dent on the right crown is one of nine such impact marks. The lines of small holes at the edge of the helmet were for attaching a lining. (Phoebe Apperson Hearst Museum of Anthropology and the Regents of the University of California, inv. 8-4597)

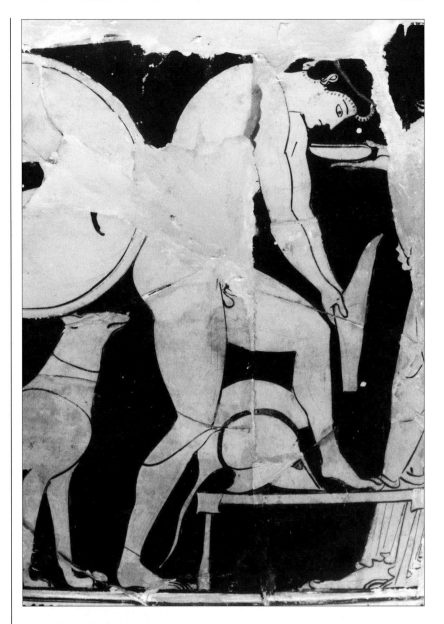

This hoplite props his leg on a stool while clipping on his greaves. It was difficult for the Greek warrior to bend down while wearing the cuirass, so the greaves were normally put on before the breastplate. His helmet rests on the stool so that it can be easily reached at the end without having to bend down. Detail from a kalyx krater (inv. G 47) decorated by the Eucharides Painter in the first decade of the 5th century BC. (Photo: M. & P. Chuzeville, Louvre, Paris)

The shins were protected by greaves. These followed the musculature of the calf and were 'clipped' on, kept in place by the natural springiness of the bronze. It was important that they fitted the leg correctly. The Hellenistic general Philopoemen remarked that a man about to leave on campaign should pay as much attention to his greaves as he did to his everyday shoes, making sure they fitted well and looked shiny (Polybius 2.9.4).

The principal offensive weapon of the hoplite was his spear (*dory*). Conquered territory was said to be 'spear-won'. In *The Persians* Aeschylus vividly portrays the Persian Wars as a contest between the oriental bow and the Greek spear.

All woods have different properties and the Greeks looked for wood which best combined strength with lightness. On vase-paintings the hoplite spear is normally shortened for artistic convenience, but is occasionally shown at its true length of up to nine feet. The remains of a 7ft 3in (2.2m) spear have been recovered from a tomb (Anderson, in *Hoplites*, p.22). Only ash could provide strong shafts of this length which were light enough to handle. Homer and Tyrtaios mention spear shafts of ash, and we may compare practice in the 'pike and shot' era when European armies of the 16th and 17th centuries AD also used ash pikes.

The properties of ash were confirmed by an experiment carried out in London by the Royal Society in AD 1663. Laths of fir, oak and ash, each one inch thick and two feet long, weighing respectively, 8, 12, and 10 ounces, were found to break when subject to weights of (respectively) 200, 250 and 325 pounds. The results demonstrated that ash gave the best combination of lightness and strength for a long infantry spear.

Ash trees could be found in the mountains of Greece, but many cities imported their supplies from Macedon or other Balkan regions. The raw material consisted of straight seasoned ash logs cut to the required length of about nine feet.

First of all the logs were split lengthways with wooden wedges and mallets. Shakes (splits) would have developed in the timber as it

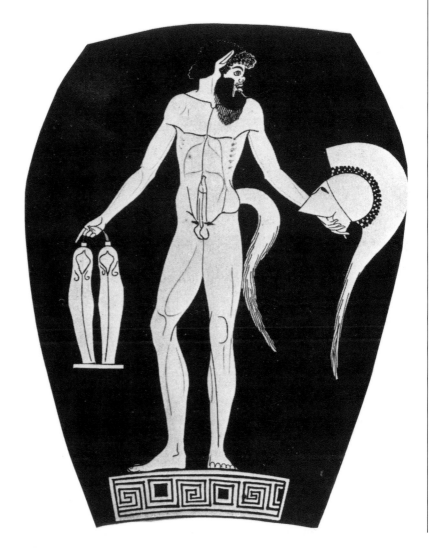

When not in use greaves were clipped onto a base and were carried by a handle. In this painting by the Kleophrades Painter, a satyr is about to hand a hoplite his greaves and helmet. (After Boardman, *Athenian Red Figure Vases. The Archaic Period* (1975) fig. 140)

seasoned. The logs were split along these shakes eliminating any weaknesses in the shafts. Splitting was repeated until the log had been divided into shafts of a couple of inches in diameter. The next stage was to shape these straight billets of wood, first with a whittling-knife (a *xuele* – shown here below in the legend of Erechthonios scene) then with rasps, until they were completely round and smooth. Consequently the spear-maker was called a *doryxoos* or 'spear-scraper' (Aristoph., *Peace* 1213) and his workshop a *doryxeion* (Hesych.).

Spear-shafts manufactured in this way tapered naturally. The point of balance of the spear was therefore not in its middle, but rather towards the butt end. Bronze or iron spear-heads and butts were produced in separate workshops. The thicker end of the shaft was fitted with the butt-spike and the narrower end with the lighter iron head. Remains of pitch have been found inside Greek spear-butts and heads, indicating the primary means of securing them to the shaft. Some spearheads or butts also have round nail-holes as a secondary means of attachment.

The final stage of production was to fit the spear with a hand-grip at its centre of balance. They are seldom illustrated but appear to be made of a square of leather wrapped around the shaft and sewn together into a sleeve.

The spear-butt was called a *styrax* or *sauroter* ('lizard-killer'). Its main purpose was to allow the spear to be planted upright in the ground

RIGHT **An Amazon hoplite swings her recurved sabre in a backhand cut. Notice the Illyrian helmet, and the deep bowl of the shield covering her shoulder. This scene on a kalyx krater was painted a little before 445 by an artist from the circle of the Penthesilea Painter. (Museo Civico Archeologico, Bologna, inv. Pell. 289)**

BELOW **This painting depicts a variant version of the legend of Erechthonios, the half-serpent son of Hephaistos who was reared by Athena. Here Herakles opens the chest containing Erechthonios and slays the serpent entwined with him with a *xuele* or whittling-knife. (M. et P. Chuzeville, Louvre, Paris, CA 1853)**

The ancient Greek falchion is rarely depicted. Here it is shown again being used in a backhand cut. The weapon was clearly borrowed from the Persians. Detail from a kylix cup in Berkeley (inv. 8.4) painted shortly after 520 by an artist in the circle of the Nikosthenes Painter. (After *Corpus Vasorum Antiquorum*, America 5, pl. 213)

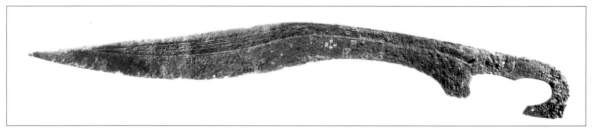

Bronze recurved sabre. The hilt sometimes ends in the shape of a bird- or animal-head, or, as in this example, curves back to guard the knuckles. (Trustees of the British Museum, Inv. 90,8–10,2)

when not in use. The *Iliad* (10.153) describes the sleeping comrades of Diomedes, heads resting on their shields, with spears upright beside them, the butt-spikes driven deep into the ground. It is claimed that the butt-spike served as a secondary head if the spear broke, but there is little evidence for this, at least for hoplite spears.

The most common type of sword used by hoplites had a cruciform hilt and a straight, double-edged, leaf-shaped blade, broadening towards the tip. In a second type, a recurved sabre resembling a kukri, the back of the blade curves forward, and the main weight of the weapon lies near the tip; the concave side forming the cutting edge. The Greeks also used a type of falchion, with a heavy single-edged blade, whose back was either straight or slightly concave. The edge has a pronounced convex curve and broadens considerably towards the point. These last two weapons came into use in the later 6th century BC, and may have been oriental in origin.

The Greeks had several names for different swords, and it is difficult to establish which terms applied to which type. The standard Greek word for sword, *xiphos*, probably referred to the straight-bladed weapon. *Kopis*, literally 'chopper', was used of the domestic meat-cleaver, and in a military context presumably covered both the falchion and the recurved sabre. Xenophon (*Eq.* 12.11) used the word *machaira* as a synonym for *kopis*, and contrasts it with the *xiphos*, so the term *machaira* was probably applied to both the recurved sabre and the falchion, but not the straight sword.

THE CAMPAIGN

Ephebes would rarely be called on to fight before their training was completed, usually only if the state was invaded and in the greatest danger. Likewise older citizens were not liable for foreign service after a certain age. In Athens the maximum age for mobilisation for foreign service was 50, but citizens could be summoned to serve at home until the age of 60. This means that at any time there were up to 42 age classes liable for mobilisation.

Mobilisation

Most Greek city-states were organised on a territorial basis, and the ultimate sub-division of the tribe was the parish, where the citizen register was maintained by the elected head of the parish. The commander of each of the tribal regiments would maintain his own register of all tribal members available for hoplite service on the basis of these parish registers.

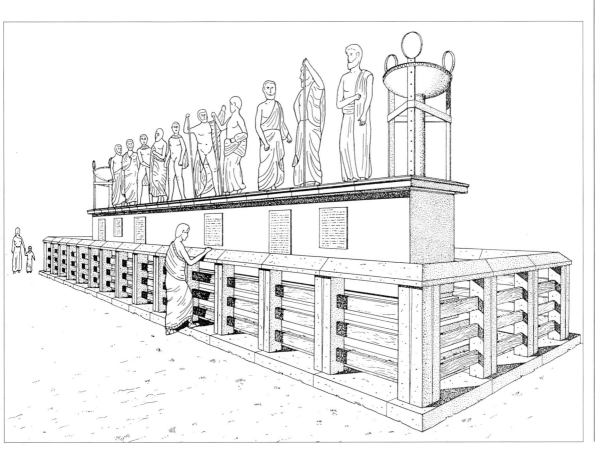

Monument to the Ten Eponymous Heroes following the reconstruction by W. B. Dinsmoor Jr. The ancient heroes from whom the ten Athenian tribes took their names were each represented by a bronze statue. Mobilisation notices for each tribe were attached below the statue of the tribe's respective hero. (Photo: American School of Classical Studies at Athens: Agora Excavations)

In all Greek states with a constitutional government matters of war and peace were debated by an assembly of all male citizens who had completed their military training. If war was decided on the assembly then had to decide how many men would be required, for how many days and how the army was to be mobilised. There were three possible methods of mobilisation:

(1) The entire people (*demos*) could be mobilised up to the maximum age of service. This type of mobilisation was called 'by the whole people' (*pandemei*) and was rarely employed.

(2) More usually an expedition of limited size and of pre-determined duration was approved. The numbers required were supplied by calculating up to which age-class the citizenry would be called out. In Athens, where each age-class was given the eponym (or title) of an Athenian hero, this type of mobilisation was called 'by eponym' (*en tois eponymois*). In Sparta the age-classes were referred to as being one, two, three etc. years past their *hêbê* (roughly translatable as 'flower of youth', meaning their first year of manhood). The mobilisation decree stated that service was required by all up to so many years from their *hêbê*.

(3) Finally, in Athens at least, the citizenry could be mobilised 'by part' (*en tois meresin*). In this system only age classes of a proportion of the tribes would be mobilised, for example for long-term service in a distant garrison. In due course this levy would be de-mobilised and replaced with the corresponding age-classes from other tribes. This rotational system enabled the Athenians to man foreign garrisons or expeditions on a long-term basis.

The mobilisation order would normally then be posted in written form. In Athens the ten commanders of the tribal regiments compiled lists by tribe of all citizens obliged to report for service, and these lists were posted in the *agora* (market-place) on the Monument of the Ten Heroes. Aristophanes (*Peace* 1180–4) describes how these 'taxiarchs' might add or delete names from the list two or three times before a campaign eventually got underway.

This kylix cup (inv. 16583) painted around 480 shows hoplites preparing to depart on campaign. On the left a hoplite and his slave boy take a shield down from the wall and out of its cover. The diminutive size of the slave boy is common in paintings of this type and reflects social status rather than age. On the right a hoplite is either wiping the dust off his spear, or rubbing it with wax or oil. (Direzione Generale Musei Vaticani, Vatican City)

In modern times only a proportion of young males are conscripted for military training, often as little as 40 percent, and even in time of war the majority of adult males remain at home, either on account of age, physical condition or occupation. In ancient Greece conscription and mobilisation were effectively universal, citizens enjoying the benefits of freedom in exchange for their obligation to defend the state. Since campaign seasons were short (at least at the beginning of the Classical period) slaves, old men and teenagers could look after the animals and crops while the men were away fighting. Most Greek states, to a greater or lesser extent, relied on slavery. A few states like Athens also had a small citizen population of urban poor, who were exempt from military service on land, but Athens was not a typical Greek state. In most Greek states a citizen was a soldier and therefore a hoplite.

Some citizens were exempt from military service as a result of physical infirmity. A surviving Athenian court speech (Lysias 24) indicates that crippled and sickly citizens could register to receive a dole, and that persons on this register were examined annually by the Council. Presumably such citizens were also excused from military service. Such cases were, however, exceptional. Spartan citizens were liable for military service even when lame; indeed, the famous Spartan warrior-king Agesilaos suffered from this ailment. Plutarch (*Mor.* 217 C) preserves the story of the Lakedaimonian Androkleidas who enrolled himself on the register of those fit to fight, even though he had a crippled leg. When turned down, he protested: 'I do not have to be able to run away, but rather to stand and fight the foe'.

Departure on campaign

On discovering that he had been mobilised the hoplite returned home to make the necessary preparations. First he prepared his weapons. In

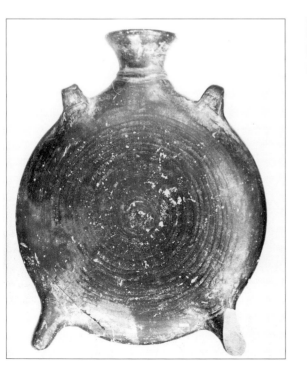

This hoplite's water canteen, found in Athens and probably dating to the 4th century BC, is surprisingly modern in appearance. It would have been covered with diagonal leather straps and lined round the edge. Note the holes through the lugs, which allow attachment to a shoulder sling. (Kiel Kunsthalle, Antikensammlung, inv. B61.1906)

The Acharnians (1071–1142) Aristophanes describes the preparations made by the Athenian general Lamachus before he departed on campaign. It was usual to hang weapons on the walls and above the fireplace (57, 278). These weapons were often covered to protect them from dust. The colour of the dyed plumes and crests would fade if displayed with the helmets, so they were usually stored separately in special boxes (1109).

The mobilisation order usually stated how much food was to be carried, for example 'three days rations' for a short campaign (197). As campaigns became longer, it became necessary for governments to provide food or a ration allowance. Military pay was probably introduced in Athens in 462, and other states were forced to follow suit. The rations, salt (perhaps flavoured with thyme), onions, salt-fish wrapped in fig-leaves, were carried in a wicker pannier called a *gylion*. Iron spits were taken for roasting fresh meat acquired on campaign.

Each hoplite was accompanied by a personal attendant. Several names are given to these auxiliaries, most frequently *skeuophoroi*, 'baggage-carriers'. They were usually slaves. Slavery was common in Greece, especially in the more urbanised city-states such as Athens, where most citizens had a personal slave. On occasion, hoplites took younger relatives with them on campaign (Isaios 5.11). These attendants carried the hoplite's provisions, bedding and personal kit, and gathered firewood, forage and water and cooked the meals for the hoplites. When the army was on the march and not under immediate threat they might also carry the hoplite's shield. In a scene that is perhaps more comic than true to life, Aristophanes has the general Lamachus tie his bedding to his shield and hand it over to his baggage-carrier while he carries the *gylion* basket. They left the ranks only when the phalanx formed up immediately before advancing to battle.

On the narrow country roads of Greece the hoplite and his attendant would normally march *eis duo*, or two abreast. If close to the enemy the

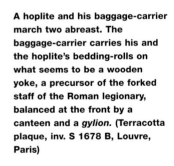

A hoplite and his baggage-carrier march two abreast. The baggage-carrier carries his and the hoplite's bedding-rolls on what seems to be a wooden yoke, a precursor of the forked staff of the Roman legionary, balanced at the front by a canteen and a *gylion.* (Terracotta plaque, inv. S 1678 B, Louvre, Paris)

An ox-cart with two solid wheels, from a monument commemorating a benefactor who gave grain (presumably including the cart's contents) to the city of Ephesus. Detail from a sculpture in the British Museum. (GR1874.7–10.324, Author's photo)

20

attendants might move to the rear. Heavier equipment would be carried in waggons. Xenophon (*Cyr.* 6. 2. 34) recommends that each should contain a shovel and mattock, as well as spare timbers to repair any damage to the cart itself. Each pack-animal should carry an axe and a sickle. These recommendations probably reflect Lakedaimonian practice. In another work (*Lak. Pol.* 11.2) he notes that when mobilised the Lakedaimonian army was accompanied by craftsmen, and that the army's implements were to be carried partly in carts and partly on baggage animals. Other tools, such as saws, were required for constructing field works. Baskets for moving earth were generally carried in pairs over the shoulder, suspended from a pole.

THE HOPLITE BATTLE

There was no 'typical' hoplite battle, each one differed in significant details. Nevertheless in what follows I have tried to give a picture of the various stages of an encounter between two hoplite armies, ignoring the role played by cavalry and light infantry and the changes in hoplite tactics over time.

Deployment into line

The Greeks ate two main meals during the day: breakfast (*ariston*) which was eaten in the mid-morning, and dinner (*deipnon*) which was an evening meal (e.g. Xen., *An.* 4.6.21–22). Hoplite battles would normally be fought in the middle of the day, after both sides had taken their mid-morning meal, which normally included wine. The ancient Greeks, like their modern counterparts, were moderate drinkers, but there was a tendency to take an extra nip before battle to steady the nerves. The commanders made their final preparations for battle over breakfast and decided on the watchword for the day. Xenophon (*Hell.* 6.4.8) comments that the Spartan king Kleombrotos and his colleagues drank too much during the last council before the battle of Leuktra.

After breakfast, the hoplite army marched out of camp, probably in column, and drew up in line of battle. The baggage-carriers remained behind in the camp, along with the army's carts and baggage-animals. Any soldiers beyond the age of military service accompanying the expedition would also be left behind in camp. At the battle of Mantineia, the Mantineians and a thousand Argive picked troops broke through a gap in the Spartan line and reached the camp, where they killed some of the older men stationed with the carts (Thuc. 5.72.3).

Once formed in line, the hoplites rested their shields against their knees, and their spears upright on the ground. The shield weighed 6.2kg (13.5 pounds) or more, heavy enough to become uncomfortable if supported for long on the forearm. The Spartan punishment for insubordination was to stand sentry all day with shield on arm (Xen., *Hell.* 3.1.9), an ancient equivalent of modern pack-drill.

The watchword was now made known to the troops. Xenophon (*An.* 1.8.16) describes how at the battle of Cunaxa in 401 the watchword 'Zeus Saviour and Victory' was passed along the hoplite line, from the right where the general was stationed to the left, and then back down the line again. This was to ensure that all had heard the phrase

This hoplite rests his shield against his knees. He wears a decorated tunic of heavy material, perhaps a *spolas*. Note also the head-band, worn to reduce helmet chafing. The lion, an enduring symbol of bravery, was a common Greek shield device. Detail from an Attic red-figured pelike of *c.*440–430 decorated by the Kleophon Painter. (Courtesy, Museum of Fine Arts, Boston, © 1999, inv. 03.793)

correctly. As with modern passwords the watchword was in two halves, the challenge and the reply, which were clear, logically connected, but not obvious.

The advance

Xenophon (*An.* 2.2.18) uses the term *ephodos* for the advance of the phalanx. The older, more experienced men in the rear ranks now came into their own. Like the NCOs of a modern army they kept the line moving forward and made sure nobody dropped out. There would be much shouting and calling by name as troops got too far ahead in some places and fell behind in others. Few Greek armies were capable of advancing in line over any great distance without becoming disordered. It was the disciplined advance of the Spartans, perhaps the only ones capable of marching in step, which made them such a formidable foe. They would march slowly and in step to the tune of a flute 'not for any religious reason, but in order that they might march up with even step and keeping time without breaking their ranks, a thing which large armies often do as they close with the enemy' (Thuc. 5.70).

Thucydides makes it clear that most armies had great difficulty advancing with their ranks in good order. Any unexpected obstacle could bring the phalanx to a complete halt or break its formation. Aristotle (*Pol.* 5.2.12) notes that the phalanx would break up if it were forced to cross even the smallest water-course. As a result generals selected plains on which to fight their battles, otherwise most hoplite armies would simply find it impossible to come to contact. At the battle of Cunaxa, fought on a flat plain, Xenophon (*An.* 1.8.18) notes that during the advance part of the line billowed forward, and those left behind had to break into a run to catch up. The distance which a hoplite line had to cover during the advance was also important. In one of the battles of the Sicilian campaign the Syracusan general Diomilos advanced his troops as quickly as he could against the Athenians, but after marching 25 *stadia* (about 7 or 8 km) they reached the Athenian line in considerable disorder and were quickly defeated, Diomilos being killed along with half his force (Thuc. 6.97.3–4).

This well-trained sub-unit, a half-file of eight men, marching in step with spears sloped over the right shoulder, may be a mercenary contingent, drilled perhaps by a Lakedaimonian officer. The fifth soldier from the left turns his head to the right, as if about to give orders. Detail from the Nereid Monument of Xanthus now in the British Museum. (Author's photo)

The formation often broke up during the advance. When asked by Socrates to define a brave man, the Athenian general Laches replied 'Whoever is willing to stand fast in his rank and resist the enemy and not run away' (Plato, *Laches* 190 e). But not all men were courageous. Theophrastus (*Char.* 25) sketches a stock character, 'the coward', who claims that he must go back to his tent because he has forgotten his sword, or carries a wounded colleague back to camp on his back for treatment, looks after him, sponges his wound and keeps the flies away, anything rather than go back to the line. Covered in blood he will explain how he saved the life of a friend at the risk of his own, showing the members of his tribe and parish the wounded man when they return to the camp.

Fear often destroyed a hoplite line long before it reached the enemy. In 397 the Lakedaimonian general Derkylidas was leading his allied army towards Ephesus when they unexpectedly came across the enemy (*Hell.* 3.2.17). He ordered the various contingents to form up eight deep. The mercenary contingents from the Peloponnese quietly prepared for battle, 'but as for the men from Priene and Achilleion, and the men from the Islands, and the Ionian cities, some of them left their arms in the standing corn, for the corn grew tall in the plain of the Maeander, while those who did stand showed clearly that they would not stand very long'. In this case fear led the hoplites of one side to run away before the advance had even started.

The signs of nervousness in a formation were obvious to the experienced eye, even from a distance. At Amphipolis in 422 the Spartan general Brasidas commented of his Athenian enemy: 'Those men will not stand up to us. They show it by the movement of their spears and their heads. Men who act in this way will never await the charge of their opponents' (Thuc. 5.10.5).

In the vast majority of hoplite battles the two sides never actually came to contact. One side stumbled to a halt and melted away long before the final charge, as research tells us was also the case in the Napoleonic Wars. Many Greek generals are recorded as pleading with their men to 'Grant me one step forward and we will have victory' (Polyaenus 2.3.2; 3.9.27; 4.3.8). No doubt this is what happened when many a hoplite line stopped advancing.

The depth of the phalanx was an important factor in determining if a formation would fight or not. It was the job of hoplites at the back, who were in no immediate danger, to push forward those in front of them. Hoplites in the front ranks were physically unable to run away, since they could not push back through the rear ranks. It was usually a loss of confidence of the men in the rear ranks which caused a hoplite line to break: faltering phalanxes collapsed from the back not the front.

There was a tendency to make the hoplite file deeper and deeper, giving the men in the rear ranks a greater feeling of security. This was especially true of the Thebans, who drew their phalanx up 25 ranks deep at the battle of Delion (Thuc. 4.93.4) and 'exceedingly deep' at the battle of the Nemea River (Xen., *Hell.* 4.2.18). Modern commentators talk of the 'weight' or 'momentum' of the deep phalanx, but this is a false perception.

Providing that both advancing armies had kept their nerve, the hoplites of both sides would start to sing the 'paean', when they were

about three or four *stadia* apart (Xen., *An.* 1.8.17: the *stadion* measured 600 feet). The paean was a hymn summoning the aid of Enyalios, the god of battle. The soldiers of different states sang variants of the paean in their own dialects. Thucydides (7.44.6) describes how the Athenian army, Ionian by race, was once thrown into confusion when their Dorian allies began to sing the paean. Their Syracusan enemy was also Dorian by race, and its paean would have been similar.

With the two hoplite lines rapidly approaching each other, a sacrifice (*sphagia*) was performed shortly before the trumpeter gave the signal to charge (Thuc. 6.69.2). Each city-state had their own preferred type of offering, sacrificed to different gods or goddesses. Xenophon (*Hell.* 4.2.20) notes that at the battle of the Nemea River the Lakedaimonians 'as is their custom' sacrificed a goat to Artemis Agrotera ('of the wild'). This they did when only one *stadion* distant from the enemy, and then charged.

The charge

The Greek word for this phase of battle was *epidromê*. Xenophon (*Hell.* 4.3.17) confirms that the trumpet signal for the charge would generally be given when both sides were about a *stadion* (600 feet) apart.

The hoplite line then broke into a run and roared out their battle-cry. Aristophanes (*Birds* 364) renders this as 'eleleleu'. Screams are difficult to transcribe. Its effect must have been like the Russian 'hurrah' or the Confederate rebel yell. The poet Aeschylus (*Ag.* 49), who fought at Marathon along with his brother Kynegiros (who was killed), compared the noise to the scream of eagles.

In the final stages of this dash to contact, the hoplite would have adjusted the position of his weapons. His shield, normally carried sideways on the left side, and somewhat at an angle, would now have been swung forwards to cover as much of his body as possible. Euripides (*Troades* 1197–9) has Hecuba describe the rim of her husband Hector's shield as stained with the sweat from his brow as he pressed his beard against the shield's rim. The precise method in which the spear was held has provoked enormous debate. Hoplites are shown holding the spear in both the underarm and overarm position.

The precise timing of the signal for the charge relied on the judgement of the general. If given too soon the hoplites would be exhausted by the run and the line would lose coherence. If given too late the hoplite line would fail to gain momentum. It was also

This Archaic Cypriot limestone statue of the three-bodied giant Geryon gives an idea of how hoplites 'locked shields' during the final stages of the advance to contact. (Metropolitan Museum of Art, New York, inv. 74.51.2591)

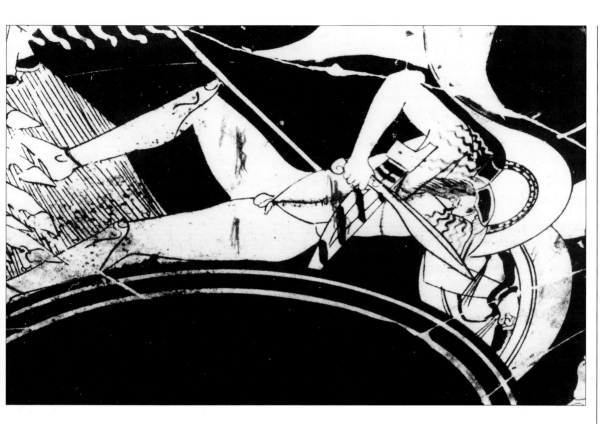

This hoplite, a giant fighting with the goddess Athena, has fallen and been wounded in both thighs, left undefended between his shield and greaves, by the jabbing spear of his opponent. He has drawn his recurved sabre from its distinctive sheath. Detail from a kylix cup decorated by the Brygos Painter c.490. (Jutta Tietz-Glagow, Antikensammlung, Staatliche Museen zu Berlin – Preussischer Kulturbesitz, Berlin, F2293)

advantageous to be the first side to deliver the charge. The Athenian general Iphicrates believed this to be particularly important (Polyaenus 3.9.26). The sound of thousands of men bellowing their battle-cry, the noise of bronze armour and weapons clattering together, and the sight of a line of hoplites running at them, was often just enough to unnerve the enemy line and make them turn and run.

If the enemy turned and ran they would be speedily overtaken by the charging troops and would suffer heavy losses. At the so-called 'tearless battle' fought in 368, the charge of the Lakedaimonians was so terrifying that few of the Arcadian enemy waited until they came within spear-thrust. Those who did were quickly killed, and the remainder were cut down as they fled. Not one Lakedaimonian died in the action (Xen., *Hell.* 7.1.31–3).

Mêlée

If the two sides did meet, then the two lines of shields clashed against each other, as each side physically tried to push the other back (Thuc. 4.96.2). The shield often buckled as a result of this violent impact. When the slave Daos recovered the body of his master from the field his shield was so badly bent that the enemy had not bothered to strip it from the body (Men., *Aspis* 72–3). Hoplites in the rear ranks gave support by pushing forward those in front with their shields (Asclepiodotus 5.2).

Then there began what Sophocles (*Ant.* 670) described as the 'storm of spears' when hoplites had to remain 'true and noble standing at each other's side'. Experienced hoplites aimed for undefended parts of the enemy's body above and below the shield, jabbing at them rapidly and repeatedly with their spears.

27

The throat, groin and thighs were especially vulnerable. In a battle in 365 the Spartan king Archedamos was immediately wounded through the thigh when his hoplite line closed with the Arcadians (Xen., *Hell.* 7.4.23). An anecdote preserved by Plutarch (*Mor.* 241 F) mentions a Spartan who was forced to crawl on all fours, after battle wounds rendered him unable to walk. The Spartan poet Tyrtaios mentions the sight of an older hoplite spilling out his spirit in the dust, clutching his wounded groin, his face white against his grey beard.

The spear-shaft often shattered at the first blow (Aeschylus, *Ag.* 64–6). Once his spear was broken the hoplite drew his sword. Plutarch (*Tim.* 28.1; *Pyrrh.* 7.5) states that skill rather than strength was required when the spear-fighting or *doratismos* was over and it came to fighting with swords. The Athenian general Nikias noted that those who had paid for extra individual weapon training from the *hoplomachoi* now reaped the benefit, when the ranks had broken and one had to fight man to man (Plato, *Laches* 182 A).

The fighting could become very confused. At the battle of the River Nemea in 394 the Lakedaimonians swiftly overcame their adversaries on the right flank, but their allies on the opposite flank did not stand and fight 'all except the men of Pellene who happened to be opposite the Thespians. Both sides fought and held their ground' (Xen., *Hell.* 4.2.20).

The Thespians had fought with equal gallantry some 30 years earlier at the battle of Delion in 424. The Boeotian line had collapsed on the left wing, all except the Thespians who stood and fought. The Athenian line bent and circled round the Thespians 'and some of the Athenians too, being disordered as they surrounded the enemy, were unable to recognise their countrymen, and killed each other' (Thuc. 4.96.3). Eventually, the Thespians were cut down fighting hand to hand.

State shield blazons were first used in the 5th century BC, but became universal only in the 4th, so visual recognition was practically impossible, since the hoplites of both sides purchased their arms privately. The watchword was a key method of recognition in the mêlée and pursuit. The commander issued the watchword immediately before the battle to keep it secret from the enemy. Thucydides (7.44.4–6) describes how the Athenians gave away their watchword when their formations became disordered during the night fighting on the Epipolai heights near Syracuse in 413. They called it out repeatedly so that their dispersed troops could regroup in the dark. The Syracusans, still in formation, overheard the answer to the watchword and used it to surprise and kill the Athenians in large numbers.

At this stage in our examination of the hoplite battle we might pause and consider what motivated the hoplite to fight, rather than run. Ultimately it was loyalty to the people who knew him at home. In the Athenian army members of the same parish served in the same company (*lochos*) and similar systems of territorial mobilisation were employed in practically all Greek city-states. Fathers and sons, nephews and uncles, cousins and boyhood friends, all fought alongside one another. Socrates, a veteran of the battles of Potidaea, Amphipolis and Delion, comments that once stationed in the line a hoplite must remain and run his risks, as neither death nor any other fate is more disgraceful than flight (Pl., *Ap.* 28 D). If a hoplite ran away, he would be reminded of it by his relatives and neighbours until the end of his life.

Pursuit

If an army broke not everyone joined in the rout. When the Athenian phalanx broke at Delion, the philosopher Socrates gathered together a small group of comrades and retreated steadily as a formed band although 'the enemy were pressing them hard and killing many'. At Potidaea Socrates saved the life of Alcibiades by standing over his wounded body and with the most conspicuous bravery defending him 'armour and all' (Plut., *Alc.* 7.3–4). The last point is stressed: it was normal to strip a wounded hoplite to lighten the load when carrying him from the battlefield.

When an army broke the results could be dramatic. Thucydides (5.72.4) notes how at Mantineia in 418 most of the allied army fled at once without waiting to come to blows with the Lakedaimonians 'and some were even trodden under foot in their hurry to escape being overtaken by the enemy'. Xenophon (*Hell.* 4.4.11–2) describes how at the battle of the (Corinthian) Long Walls a group of panic-stricken Argives became trapped and were slaughtered by the Lakedaimonians against the city walls of Corinth, crushed, trodden under foot by one another, and suffocated, making no attempt to defend themselves. 'So many fell within a short time that men accustomed to see heaps of corn, wood, or stones beheld then heaps of dead bodies.'

Casualties among the army which broke its ranks first were disproportionately large. According to calculations made by Krentz ('Casualties in Hoplite Battles' *Greek, Roman and Byzantine Studies* 26 (1985) 13-20), the number of dead on a Greek battlefield averaged 5% of the victors and around 14% of the defeated. During the night battle at Syracuse in 413 the Athenians lost as many as 20–25% of their force.

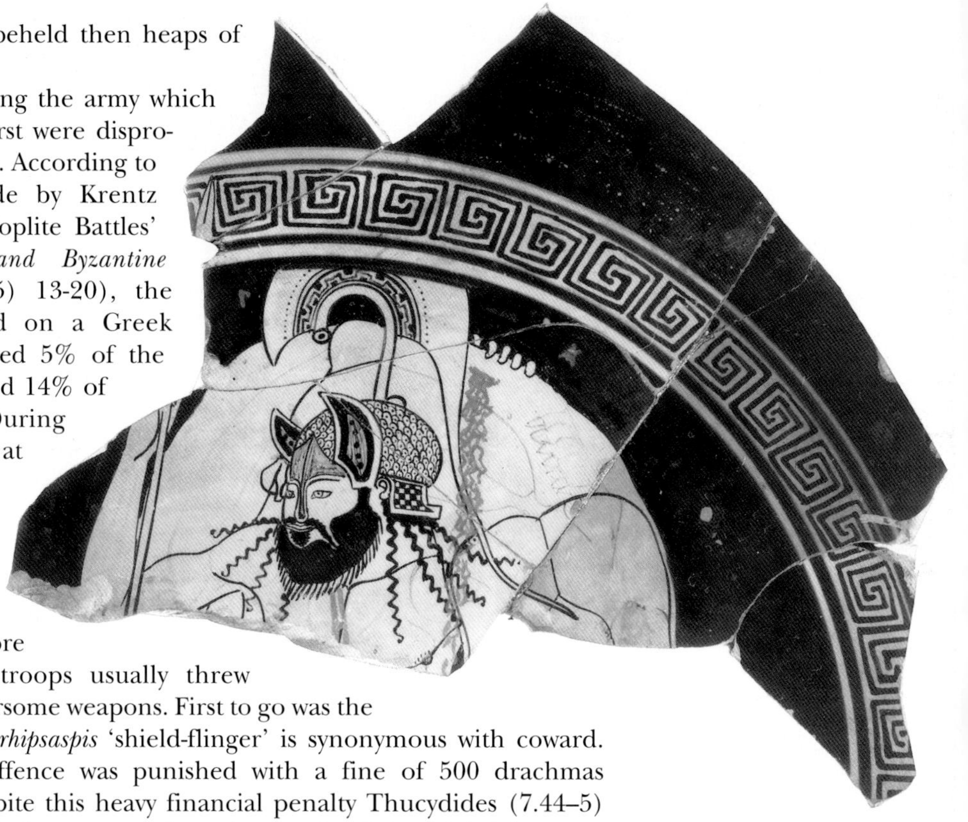

To escape more quickly, fleeing troops usually threw away their cumbersome weapons. First to go was the shield: the word *rhipsaspis* 'shield-flinger' is synonymous with coward. In Athens the offence was punished with a fine of 500 drachmas (Lys. 10.13). Despite this heavy financial penalty Thucydides (7.44–5) reports that in the desperate night action on the Epipolai heights near Syracuse the Athenian hoplites left behind an immense quantity of shields and other arms, as they attempted to climb down the rocky bluffs to safety. In practice it proved impossible to introduce and enforce clear legislation to punish 'shield-flinging'. The distinction between throwing arms in rout, or losing them in action or in accidental mishaps was blurred. Plato discusses the problem in his *Laws* (944).

It was important for the victors to keep formation as they chased the enemy, who might have been victorious on the other wing. Clouds of dust rising from the dry soil of the plain often obscured one side of the battlefield from the other. At Cunaxa when the enemy line broke the victors conducted the pursuit with great energy, but shouted to one another not to run ahead at breakneck pace, and to keep their ranks (Xen., *An.* 1.8.19). The recall from the pursuit was signalled by a blast on the trumpet (Xen., *An.* 4.2.22). Krentz (in *Hoplites*, p.114–6) has identified six different trumpet calls used by hoplite armies.

Aftermath

When the pursuit was over the victors returned to look after their wounded and to gather their dead. Then they stripped the enemy bodies, first of their armour, and then of their clothing and any jewellery, such as finger-rings. Booty was normally pooled. Generals had often vowed to dedicate a tenth of the booty to a particular god if he granted victory. The rest might be given to 'booty-sellers' who auctioned it to raise money for the state, or was simply divided among the troops. Some of the captured armour would be used to erect a trophy (*tropaion*) at the point where the 'turn round' (*trope*) of the enemy had first occurred.

Ajax carries the body of Achilles from the battlefield over his shoulders in a 'fireman's lift'. Achilles has died from a bleeding gash in his abdomen rather than a wound in the heel. Ajax, whose face is depicted in almost 'Japanese' style, wears a Chalcidian helmet of composite construction. From two fragments of a kylix cup (frg. 537 & 598) by Douris. (Cabinet des Médailles, Paris)

RIGHT **A hoplite panoply, spoil taken from the enemy, is shown here nailed to a tree trunk, as a 'trophy' or memorial of battle. Nike, the goddess of victory, drills a hole to hang up the shield. The artist who painted this pelike is called the Trophy Painter after this, his 'name vase'. (Courtesy, Museum of Fine Arts, Boston, © 1999, inv. 30.187)**

Usually it was nailed to a nearby tree as a monument of the battle. Some of the balance would be dedicated to the gods, either at a local sanctuary or at one of the great Pan-Hellenic centres. It has been estimated that about 100,000 helmets were dedicated at Olympia alone during the 7th and 6th centuries BC. Herodotus (8.27.4) tells us that after a single victory over the Thessalians the Phocians dedicated 2,000 captured shields at Delphi and 2,000 at Abai (A. M. Snodgrass, *Archaic Greece* (1980) 131).

The defeated city sent out its herald to request a truce to bury their dead. According to the customs of war this constituted an admission of defeat, and so was rarely refused. The request was made as quickly as possible so the bodies could be buried before they began to putrefy or were eaten by scavenging animals. Normally the bodies were buried together in a mass grave on the battlefield. This must have been a grim task after the battle of Delion, for the Athenian dead lay on the battlefield for over 17 days before the Boeotians granted permission for burial (Thuc. 4.101.1). Even after three days in the sun faces could become so bloated that identification was difficult (Men., *Aspis* 69–72).

The fallen were listed by tribe alongside their relatives and neighbours in a casualty list commissioned by the state and erected in the centre of the city. Such tribal casualty lists are known from a number of Greek states. Sometimes an elaborate empty tomb, or cenotaph, was erected in the city to commemorate the sacrifice of its citizens, and a funeral oration was commissioned to celebrate their patriotism.

The wounded could take a long time to die. Greek medical writings contain some lurid descriptions of the symptoms of fatal battle wounds. The Hippocratic treatise *On Wounds in the Head* (19) describes the grim

Each Greek state had a herald who was inviolate even in time of war. He was placed under the protection of Hermes, the messenger of the gods, and carried the wand and hat of the god as symbols of his inviolability. This skyphos (inv. G 146), painted by Makron at the end of the 6th century BC, shows Talthybios, the herald of Agamemnon and the Greeks during the Trojan War. To the left Agamemnon leads Briseis away from the tent of Achilles. (Photo: P. Lebaube, Louvre, Paris)

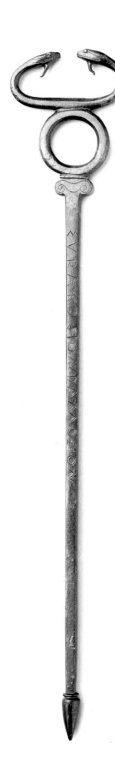

A bronze herald's wand or *kerykeion*, inscribed as 'belonging to the state of the Syracusans'. The form of the letters suggest a date of *c.485–470*. (Museum für Kunst und Gewerbe, Hamburg)

stages in which the victim of an untreatable head-wound dies within fourteen days in winter or just seven in summer. Elsewhere (*Epidemics* 5.61) the stages of death from peritonitis over five days after an abdominal wound are described in agonising detail. Casualties sometimes lingered on for considerably longer. Hanson (p.218) has suggested that this may be why occasionally new names are added in different handwriting to the inscribed lists of the fallen.

Hoplites were proud to have survived being wounded in battle. The Athenian taxiarch Nikomachides shows Socrates his scars to demonstrate how unjust it was of the Athenians not to elect him general, after he had served as a company and regimental commander, and had been wounded in action so many times (Xen., *Mem.* 3.4.1).

THE STRATEGY OF DEVASTATION

It seems paradoxical that hoplite warfare took place in the plains of Greece, instead of the mountains. Guerrilla war would seem to be a more natural form of conflict in what is an exceptionally mountainous country. The Persian Mardonius believed that the Greeks pursued their unique style of warfare out of ignorance and stupidity:

For when they have declared war against one another, having found out the fairest and most level piece of ground, they go down into it and fight, so that the conquerors depart with great losses, to say nothing of the defeated who are entirely wiped out … if they must go to war with one another, they would do better to search out a place where they are each least likely to be subdued and fight there. (Hdt. 7.9)

One reason why the Greeks fought in this apparently suicidal manner was the limited financial resources available to the average city-state. It cost the state little to require its citizens to equip themselves with armour and weapons and to make them liable for service in time of war. In order to develop efficient missile troops, light infantry, or cavalry, the state had to compensate its citizens for the extra time spent in training, and for the purchase of specialist equipment (such as a horse). Most city-states did not have the funds to meet such expenses. Systems of state finance were relatively primitive, and the citizen body was reluctant to vote for extra taxation necessary to support a diversified army.

Until the 5th century BC only the armies of the Boeotian and Thessalian Leagues possessed anything more than a token force of cavalry. These two lowland areas were the only ones with landowners rich enough to maintain horses. Before the (medieval) invention of the horse-collar, the motive power of the horse was not put to agricultural use: ploughing fields and pulling waggons were jobs for yoked oxen. Horses were an indecently expensive form of transport and a means of social display. Many noble family fortunes were squandered in indulging the passion for horses. The beginning of Aristophanes' *Clouds* has Strepsiades counting up the debts which have mounted up paying for his son Pheidippides' mounts along with their chariots and fodder. Meanwhile Pheidippides is dreaming horses.

Athens was able to develop a cavalry force in the later 5th century BC thanks to the revenues of her growing empire. The Athenians enacted legislation to compensate cavalrymen if their horses were killed on

33

The 'Mourning Athena' of about 460 reads a list of the fallen hoplites of her patron city. (Acropolis Museum, Athens inv. 695)

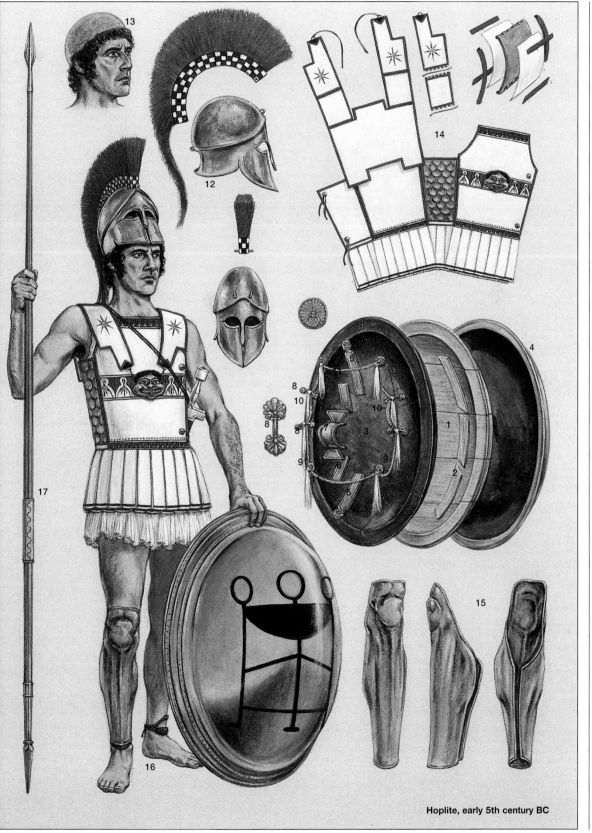

Hoplite, early 5th century BC

B

Ephebic training

Departure on campaign

C

Naval service and transport

The strategy of devastation

E

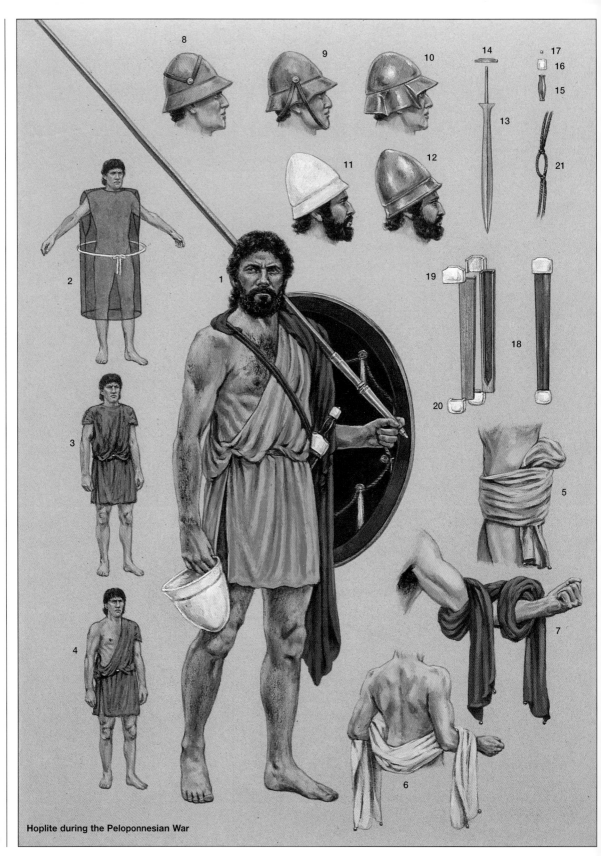

Hoplite during the Peloponnesian War

F

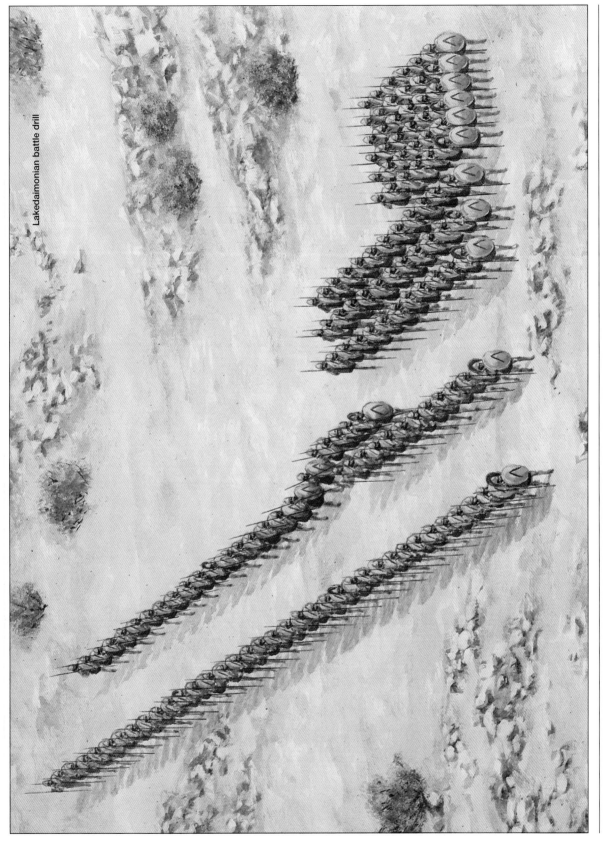

Lakedaimonian battle drill

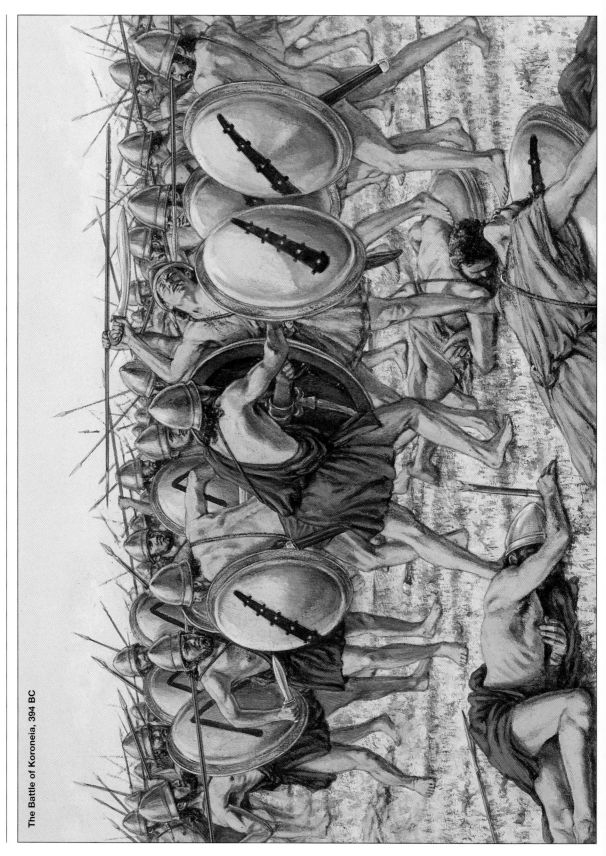

The Battle of Koroneia, 394 BC

H

The aftermath of battle

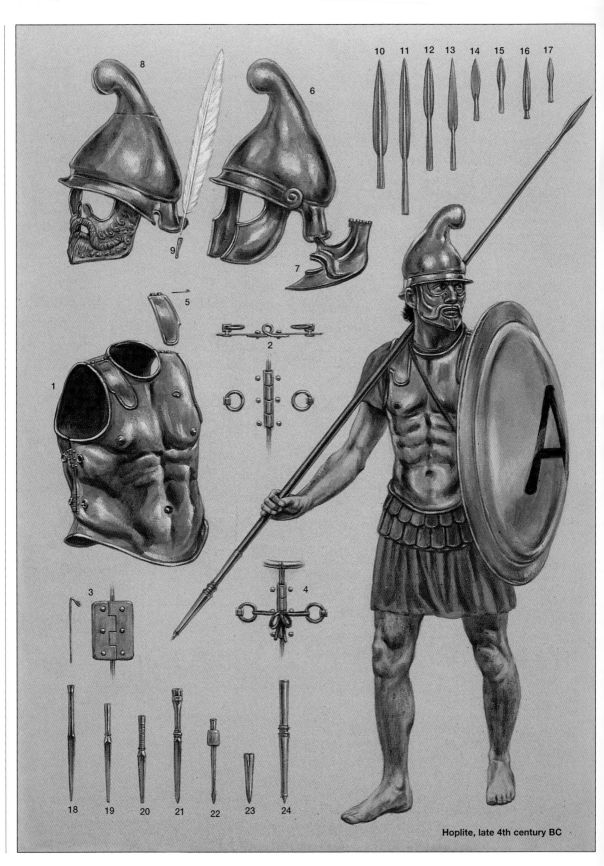

Hoplite, late 4th century BC

campaign, and the state paid an allowance for fodder, not just in time of war, but on a permanent basis. Sparta and Corinth are the only other Greek states known to have possessed forces of cavalry before the close of the 5th century BC. Most states established cavalry contingents only in the 4th century BC.

Light infantry was thought to be of little value. Early hoplite armies were accompanied by varying numbers of poorer citizens who fought as light infantry *(psiloi)*, but these troops had little effect on the course of the battle. To be effective light infantry had to be given special equipment and training. For example an effective corps of archers could only be raised by purchasing the necessary archery equipment and paying for continuous and intensive training.

In the 6th century BC archery had played an important part in Greek warfare. The tyrants who had ruled then possessed the personal wealth necessary to maintain corps of specialist troops. The Athenian Peisitratid dynasty recruited a corps of Scythian mercenary archers, while Polycrates tyrant of Samos raised a corps of archers locally. The end of the tyrants brought about a return to the deadlock of hoplite warfare.

Lack of state finances also had a major impact on the length of time an army could remain in the field. Greek hoplites were largely farmers, and were understandably reluctant to leave their land unattended for long periods. They would only vote in favour of short campaigns. Most states were in no position to provide cash to buy food and to compensate the hoplite for his absence from the farm. Consequently they would not vote for longer campaigns. Greek generals were therefore forced to adopt military strategies which would achieve the political objectives in as short a time as possible. Siege warfare was no answer to this problem.

The history of siege warfare is characterised by alternating periods when defensive or offensive techniques dominate. In the Classical period defence had almost total supremacy. Cities were ringed by colossal fortifications which were all but impregnable. The principle siege weapon was the battering-ram. The ram could make a breach in a wall or gate if a weak point could be found, but the party operating the ram was always exposed to attack, and risked prohibitive casualties. An army might try to capture a city by escalade, making a surprise attack on its walls at the beginning of the campaign; but such attempts could be extremely costly if the defender was well prepared. In effect an invading army had little chance of taking the enemy city by storm.

To take a city by investment the invader had to sit outside its walls for months if not years until the food ran out. First, the place had to be circumvallated: a ditch was dug and a rampart erected around the besieged city, then the rampart had to be constantly manned to prevent food entering the city. Circumvallation was not an option for most Greek states, since they were unable to support an army in the field for the necessary length of time.

A somewhat quicker method was to construct a siege-mound. The first siege-mound known within the Aegean area was one constructed by the Lydian king Alyattes against Smyrna around 600. The Persians later made effective use of siege-mounds to reduce many fortified cities to their rule. These were rich and populous empires which could afford the resources necessary to construct siege mounds, which required the

Scythian mercenary archers in the service of the Peisistratid tyrants of Athens shoot from the cover of a rank of kneeling hoplites. The balls are sun symbols sacred to Apollo and the wine-cup is sacred to Dionysos. (Amphora F 1865, Staatliche Museen, Berlin)

fielding of a considerable army for quite a considerable length of time, and which remained beyond the resources of most Greek states.

Sparta was something of an exception. Her hoplites were able to stay in the field practically indefinitely, because their livelihoods were guaranteed by a serf-class, who tilled their land-holdings. In the opening stages of the Peloponnesian War the Spartans took the city of Plataea after a long siege by circumvallating it and constructing a siege-mound. Until efficient siege artillery was introduced in the mid 4th century BC, other Greek states generally lacked the resources to conduct sieges on such a scale.

The usual goal of an offensive campaign was to force the defender into battle in the open as quickly as possible. The key problem was to discourage him from retiring behind the safety of his city walls with his livestock. The so-called 'strategy of devastation' was developed to force the defender out of his city. When an invader reached the plain of the enemy state – its prime agricultural asset – he sought to do as much damage to it as possible. For maximum effect, cities were usually invaded immediately before the harvest season, when the crops were still in the fields. The invader did his best to spoil the crops, or to gather them in for his own use. He would also ring-bark or otherwise damage fruit and olive trees. On occasion invaders stripped country houses of their tiles and roof beams and took them back to their own lands across the border (*Hell. Oxyrh.* 17. 4). Xenophon (*Hell.* 4.6.5) describes how in 389 the Spartan king Agesilaos advanced at snail's pace, ten to twelve *stadia* (each 600 feet) a day, into the lands of the Acarnanians, intending to lay waste their territory thoroughly. All trees in his path were uprooted (Polyaen. 2.1.10). The mere threat of such agricultural devastation was often enough to force a city to agree to terms. In 424 the Spartan general Brasidas persuaded the city of Acanthus to revolt from Athens 'for they feared for their grapes which had not yet been gathered in' (Thuc. 4.84–8).

If the defender did not accept terms, he would be forced outside his city walls to fight for his crops. If he chose to fight, the action would unfold as a hoplite battle, and took place on the level plains near the city. If he chose not to fight then the invader would invade again the next year, and again and again, in the hope that the cumulative damage caused to the agricultural infrastructure would either force the defender out to fight, or force him to eat his seed corn, which would ultimately result in starvation.

Crops ripened significantly earlier in southern Greece than further north, giving the Spartans a permanent advantage in this 'strategy of devastation'. The Spartans could gather in their crops and then invade Attica before the Athenians could harvest theirs.

At the beginning of the Archaic period the Greek world consisted of hundreds of small, independent city-states. By the end the number had dwindled considerably. The larger city-states had expanded by taking over the territory of their smaller neighbours, partly by conquest and partly by consent. In a process of centralisation known as *synoiksm*, the importance of the core city grew, and in many cases the free population of acquired territories moved to the capital of the new state.

Eventually two neighbouring states reached their limits of expansion, usually with their natural borders separated by a disputed area of coastal or upland plain. This disputed zone became a potential source of conflict. Typically it would be declared neutral by the mechanism of dedicating the land to a local god resident in the valley, and restricting or banning the use of the land for agriculture by either side. But such compromises rarely lasted long. As one of the two states expanded in power or population, its need or greed for land grew, and it would eventually attempt to annex the border land.

The majority of Greek wars had their origin in border disputes of this type. Once again, it was the agricultural plain which was in dispute, and it would be in this plain that the battle would be fought. Had either of the protagonists instead resorted to guerrilla war in the mountains they would have given the enemy open access to the disputed ground. This was in direct contradiction to the oaths taken by ephebes, who swore not to leave their fatherland weaker than they had found it.

Sometimes the invader targeted a particular area of the defender's territory, inflicting disproportionate damage on one segment of the population. The aim was to provoke internal dissension among the defenders, forcing them to opt for open battle in order to preserve internal solidarity. In the initial stages of the Peloponnesian War the Spartan king Archidamus targeted the Plain of Acharnae outside Athens. The Acharnians formed a substantial part of the Athenian population. With the Spartans devastating the plain, groups of Athenians demanded that their general, Pericles, should

Bronze head of a battering ram dedicated at Olympia during the first half of the 5th century BC. It once tipped a massive wooden beam. The rams' heads on either side of the ram allude to the weapon's name and function. (Inv. B2360, photo after *Olympiabericht V* (1956) 75–8)

The Persian siege-mound constructed to take the Cypriot city of Paphos in 498. This preserved section fills the defensive ditch which surrounded the city. An impression of the prodigious effort required to construct a siege-mound is conveyed by this imposing archaeological monument. Note, for scale, the two figures to the left of the section. (After Franz Georg Maier, *Alt-Paphos auf Cypern* (1984) pl. II, 3)

lead them out to battle. In particular, 'the Acharnians, believing themselves to be no insignificant portion of the Athenian citizen body, as it was their land that was being devastated, became insistent for a sally' (Thuc. 2.21). Pericles, however, skilfully calmed their feelings and so avoided a struggle inside the city walls.

The most effective way of taking an enemy city was by treachery, which became more common during the 4th century BC as party politics began to split Greek communities. In the first half of the 4th century BC the Arcadian general Aeneas wrote a book called *On Siege Warfare*. This work is full of recommendations on how to guard against 'the enemy within'.

The framework outlined above to explicate hoplite warfare, the 'strategy of devastation', has recently been subjected to considerable criticism. Victor Davis Hanson has pointed out the practical difficulties involved in destroying crops, and the rarity of pitched battles. It is

argued that the 'strategy of devastation' does not adequately explain what happened in Greek hoplite warfare, and should be abandoned as a model.

Down until the Peloponnesian Wars, however, conflicts were resolved by battles not campaigns (Stephen Mitchell in ed. A.B. Lloyd, *Battle in Antiquity* (1996) 87). Pericles was the first, it seems, to recommend that his people remained behind their walls. Subsequently the 'strategy of devastation' was rarely successful in forcing the defender out to fight, but what alternative did the invader have? The strategy may not have worked well, but it was the only one available, and it was a strategy of which the ancients themselves were fully aware. We will leave the last word to Xenophon (*Mem.* 2.1.13), who has been our main guide to hoplite warfare through the pages of this book: 'the stronger party will cut the corn and fell the trees of the weaker party to make them accept slavery as an escape from war'.

The 'strategy of devastation', hoplite warfare, and the independence of the Greek city state, only came to an end with the invention of effective siege artillery between 353 and 341 by artificers working under the direction of Polyidus the Thessalian, the chief mechanic of Philip II of Macedon.

THE PLATES

In selecting the scenes and materials for the following plates an attempt has been made to reach a balance between showing hardware and military practices. The range of possible subject matter is almost limitless, and many important features of hoplite warfare have, regrettably, had to be passed over.

A: HOPLITE, EARLY 5TH CENTURY BC

The main figure in the plate has as his shield blazon a symbol of Apollo, the tripod and cauldron from which the god's priestess at Delphi delivered her prophesies. This indicates that the hoplite has put himself under the protection of the deity.

The method of construction of the hoplite shield is known from an example discovered in an Etruscan tomb, now in the Museo Gregoriano, on which our reconstruction is largely based. Less well preserved examples from Olympia and elsewhere show that Greek shields were constructed in much the same way.

1 The core of the shield was made of wooden planks about 20-30cm wide, glued together into a block. This block was carefully turned on a lathe (Aristophanes, *Birds* 491) until its shape resembled a bowl: in this case about 82cm wide and 10cm deep. The rim of this block projected about 4.5cm from the wall of the bowl and formed the basis of the shield-rim. **2** It was reinforced by wooden laminations running along the sides at right angles to the grain. The Museo Gregoriano shield was made of poplar, other shields may have been made of willow. Pliny (*HN* 16.209) notes that trees that grow in water, including poplar and willow, have the most flexible wood and so are the most suitable for making shields, as the wood draws together and 'closes up its own wound' when penetrated.

3 A thin leather lining, carefully sewn together to fit the bowl-shape of the inside of the shield, was now glued to the wooden planking, **4** and a bronze sheet, just 0.5mm thick, was then bonded onto the outside of the wooden base with pitch, forming its outer surface. This sheet was turned over the rim for about 4cm without leaving any wrinkles, cuts or overlaps in the bronze. Historical metallurgists are unable to explain how these feats of bronze-working were achieved.

The handle attachments were attached to the shield last. The main handle was the bronze arm-hole (*porpax*) at the shield's centre. This assembly generally consisted of three elements. **5** First two outer shield bands, frequently ending in palmettes running over the inside of the rim, **6** then two inner shield bands, sometimes separate from the outer ones but sometimes a single element, **7** and finally the arm-hole itself. Nearly all preserved examples of these porpakes come from temple deposits dating to the Archaic period, and are highly decorated. It is probable that they became much plainer in the Classical period, as shown here.

8 Two pairs of staples, generally with palmette finials, were now attached to either side of the inside of the shield, slightly above the centre line. **9** Then four fittings for rings, often rosette-shaped, were also attached above and below the staples. **10** Finally cords ending in tassels were attached to the finials, forming a rope handle (*antilabe*) which was grasped by the left hand. It is perhaps significant that the grain of the wooden core of the Museo Gregoriano shield runs horizontally, parallel to the forearm. **11** Other cords ending in tassels were attached to the ring fittings forming loops.

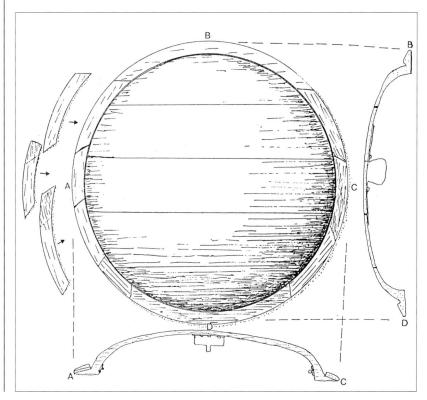

Diagram of the poplar laths which constituted the base and rim of the hoplite shield in the Museo Gregoriano. (After Henry Blyth, *Bolletino Monumenti Musei e Gallerie Pontificie* 3 (1982) 11)

Some representations of the shield show reinforcing metal bands fitted to the inside of the shield. Here one is shown running immediately behind the rim and a second one further towards the centre of the inside of the shield. Note also the plain bronze porpax and the outer bronze plating turned around the outer edge of the rim. This sherd was painted by a Greek artist working in Italy. Paestan, Workshop of Asteus, c. 350-325. (© Professor Dale Trendall)

RIGHT **The purpose of the lengths of cord fixed to the rings inside the shield is not fully understood. This Attic vase-painting of around 440 by the Lykaon Painter, shows Antimachos acting as page to the hero Neoptolemos, carrying his shield and offering him his helmet. He is using one of the loops of cord as a sling over his shoulders to help carry the shield on his back. (After Arthur Sambon,** *Collection Canessa* **no. 93)**

The most important helmet of the Archaic period had been the Corinthian helmet. It continued in popularity throughout the 5th century BC. The names given to the various types of Greek helmets are mostly misleading modern labels. However, the Greeks did call one type of helmet 'Corinthian'. Herodotus (4.180) states that during a ceremony held by a Libyan tribe the most beautiful girl wore full Greek armour and a helmet of Corinthian type. It seems reasonable to identify this helmet with the type shown first and most frequently on Corinthian pottery.

12 In the 5th century BC the Corinthian helmet evolved into a form that covered the face almost completely as the nasal and cheek-pieces moved together, and it developed a pronounced cranial ridge. An imposing horsehair crest, held in a crest-holder, was attached to the skull of the helmet. Frequently the crest-holder is decorated in a check pattern. No crest-holder has been recovered, but they were presumably made of bronze. The three bronze hoops soldered onto the skull of the helmet are based on those preserved on a somewhat earlier Corinthian helmet in Berlin. Presumably the crest-holder had catches which fitted into these hoops securing the crest to the helmet.

The increasingly uncomfortable Corinthian helmet, now without any lining, was frequently worn propped up on the top of the head before battle. **13** Sometimes hoplites are shown

ANTIMAXOS

wearing caps, worn under the helmet for comfort. This cap is based on that worn by Patroklos on a vase by the Sosias Painter. Rather than felt, the hatching seems to suggest that some woven material is being shown. Despite its elegant form the Corinthian helmet fell out of use in the Classical period because of the restrictions it placed on vision and hearing.

14 The main body of the composite cuirass normally consisted of four rectangular plates: a breast-plate and back-plate, both shaped to follow the contours of the body, and two side-plates. The breast-plate narrowed towards the top to allow the shoulders to move comfortably, and the side-plates were narrower and lower than the others, to allow for the arms. All these plates were connected by tubular hinges held together with a wire pin.

In our reconstruction, based on the cuirass from the tomb of Philip of Macedon, each shoulder-piece is made of two curved articulating sections, attached to a main section protecting the shoulders at the back and rigidly attached to the back-plate. If we were to take one of these pieces apart, we would find a metal plate beneath the linen or leather covering on both sides. The edges would be covered by a binding, often decorated in a pattern.

ABOVE **The Corinthian helmet was beaten out of a single sheet of bronze, a process requiring great skill. Greek bronze-smiths developed a high, angled 'rod' anvil specially for their production. This pyxis was painted by the Thaliarchos Painter, so called after the erotic inscriptions on vases painted by him during the final decades of the 6th century BC. (Petit Palais, Paris, inv. 382, photo after Klein,** *Lieblingsinschriften* **p.88)**

RIGHT **Before leaving the workshop the Corinthian helmet was decorated with punched and incised designs. Examples produced in Greek workshops are often furbished with eyebrows. Some of the specialist tools used are shown in this drawing of a heavily damaged and restored cup (inv. 518) in the Ashmolean Museum, Oxford, painted by the Antiphon Painter about 480. (After Furtwängler and Reichhold,** *Griechische Vasenmalerei* **III p.81)**

This type of shoulder-guard, hinged in sections, could, however, be a later development of the 4th century BC. Earlier shoulder-guards may have been made in a single piece from flexible materials. Between the shoulder-guards was a small nape-protector which projected above the back-plate.

15 Around 500 BC greaves started to imitate the anatomy of the lower leg. Some examples continue to have lines of perforations around the edge, indicating that they were lined, but this soon dies out. The greave was prised apart, taking advantage of the natural springiness of the bronze, and was clipped onto the shin.

16 Many vase paintings of this period clearly show a garter being worn underneath the bottom edge of the greave to prevent chafing. These garters would have become increasingly useful as greaves lost their linings. This example is based on that worn by Achilles as shown bandaging Patroklos by the Sosias Painter.

17 The spear would be fitted with a grip, presumably of leather. This example is based on that shown on the Achilles amphora. The wavy line along the side of the grip presumably represents the seam.

B: EPHEBIC TRAINING

Ephebes would train in publicly or privately owned *palaistrai*, buildings with an open courtyard in the centre, originally for wrestling, enclosed by wings of rooms or colonnades. The *gymnasion* was a public sports-ground, usually outside the city, provided with a *palaistra*. Here we are looking out from the *apodyterion*, or dressing-room, close to the entrance to the palaistra.

The artist who drew Achilles on this amphora around 460 is named the Achilles Painter after this, his 'name vase'. It is one of the most detailed depictions of the composite cuirass available to us, and one of the very few representations of the spear grip. It is also remarkable in showing the spear at its full length. (Direzione Generale Musei Vaticani, Vatican City)

This painting, on which Plate B is partly based, on a cup potted by Phintias, dates to a few years before 500. It was found at Tanagra and is now in the National Museum, Athens (1628). The significance of the octopus shield blazon is not fully understood. (Drawing after Pfuhl, fig. 386)

RIGHT The seven heroes arm for their march against Thebes on this kylix cup painted by Douris shortly after 500. The sequence of arming is clearly demonstrated. The third hoplite wisely puts on his greaves before his cuirass. Note the helmets of composite construction. (Kunsthistorisches Museum, Vienna, inv. 3694)

Three ephebes have just returned from practising the armoured race. Vases show athletes running with shields, greaves and helmets, and sometimes with a spear too, either without any clothing, or with an *ephaptis* (see Plate F) wrapped round their waist. Even so the genitals are usually uncovered.

1 has propped up his 'Chalcidian' helmet for comfort. The helmet is so-called since it appears earliest and most frequently on pottery once thought to originate in the Euboean city of Chalcis. Chalcis was certainly not the original home of the helmet, and 'Chalcidian' pottery may also be incorrectly attributed. The helmet softens the angular form of the Corinthian helmet, and improves vision and hearing. The cheek-pieces are rounded and the rim is indented to provide an aperture above the ear. He carries a racing shield from a set dedicated to the goddess Athena. The pentangle shield-device is formed from two superimposed archaic *alphas*. Even though shields were now faced in bronze, it is clear from the vase-paintings that in some cases the field was painted over.

2 holds his Corinthian helmet by its eye-holes in his right hand: such a hold would give some balance to the weight of the shield when running. The shield device on figure **3** shows the cock, bird of the dawn: this could imply that the ephebe was under the protection of the sun-god Helios. The cock was also an erotic symbol, however, and the young ephebe could have been given his shield as a present by an older male admirer. Figure **4**'s shield device comprises an octopus: the significance of this device is not fully

understood. Another ephebe **5** in the apodyterion is oiling and strigilating himself after training.

In the background a *hoplomachos* **6** is demonstrating how to swing up the sword for a downward cut against an opponent **7** whose spear has not yet broken. The bull was sacrificed to a large range of gods, normally by an axe blow on the neck, and the bucranium (bull's head) is a popular shield device. In Athenian contexts it is sometimes used to identify the bearer as an inhabitant of Marathon, once terrorised by a mad bull until slain by the Athenian hero Theseus. Both figures wear 'Chalcidian' helmets with hinged cheek-pieces, which made the helmet easier to put on and wear when not in action.

C: DEPARTURE ON CAMPAIGN

This scene shows two brothers as they prepare themselves for departure on campaign: their mother and sister look on tearfully. The hoplite to the left of centre puts on his cuirass: the cuirass was wrapped around the trunk and the breast-plate was secured to the left side-plate by laces tied to small bronze finials on either plate. The breast-plate can also be in two halves which fasten at the front. At this stage the two shoulder-guards would stand upright. They were pulled down in turn, and tied to either one or (more normally) two bronze finials on the breast-plate.

The sword would be put on after the cuirass. The warrior to the right of centre is wearing a bronze muscle-cuirass with unusual pteruges covered in leather scales. He cuts off a lock of his hair as a witness to a vow he has made to some

god for his safe return. Sometimes these locks of hair would be lodged in the god's temple, bound in spirals of bronze wire which are frequently found in temple excavations.

A slave (bottom right) has packed one of the two brothers' bedding rolls, rolling up all his personal kit in his mattress and packing it into the striped kit-bag, and is now packing the second. He is rolling up a small oil lamp, a drinking-mug and a shallow bowl to eat and drink from. Xenophon (*Cyr.* 6.2.26–33) gives a list of the items he believes should be taken on campaign by the perfect army. He recommends that a whittling-knife should be carried by those who know how to smooth down a replacement spear shaft, and a file to sharpen spear-heads. These items are also being packed.

Xenophon also recommends hand-mills to grind grain gathered on campaign. The one shown here is of the portable 'hopper-rubber' type found at Priene and Delos. He also advises taking medical supplies, as well as plenty of spare straps of all sizes to replace campaign breakages. Only enough wine should be taken to allow the hoplite to gradually accustom himself to drinking water alone with his dinner; a

A comic actor playing the role of a slave. He carries his master's *gylion* (here clearly of wickerwork), hooked on what is presumably a curved wooden yoke balanced on the shoulder. On his back, balanced on the other side of the yoke, is a bedding roll in a striped cover, on which hangs a haunch of venison. The object in front of the *gylion* is a *situla* or wine bucket. This slave is probably accompanying his master to a religious meal in a country shrine rather than following him on campaign. From an Apulian vase of the second quarter of the 4th century BC. (After José Dörig, *Art Antique, Collections privées de la Suisse Romande* (1975) fig. 276)

minimum of bedding and some spare clothing; and salted meats which would keep the longest. This and any other rations would be carried in the wicker *gylion*, shown here beside the mattress.

One shield is still hanging on the wall, without its cover, while the other is being polished, steadied against a shield-stand. Both shields are decorated with blazons sacred to Dionysios, a wine-cup and ivy leaves. The father has fitted on the crest to a Chalcidian helmet. Some Chalcidian helmets shown on Greek vase paintings during the first decades of the 5th century BC are made from a combination of small plates and scales rather than of a single bronze plate. The components of this helmet have been shown in iron, but could equally have been manufactured in bronze, or painted or covered in leather or fabric.

D: NAVAL SERVICE AND TRANSPORT

A fully manned 'fast' trireme had a crew of about 200. It would be propelled by 170 oarsmen rowing in three benches numbering 62, 54 and 54 each. The oarsmen seem to have rowed naked. They would either be recruited from the poorer citizens of the state unable to purchase hoplite armour, impoverished foreigners, or might be slaves pressed or induced into service. Each rower would be issued with one of three different types of oar, depending on which bench he was rowing, and would carry a loop to attach it to the thole-pin at his bench and a cushion to sit on. An oarsman is shown boarding the trireme.

The trireme also needed a dozen or so sailors to steer the ship, trim the sails etc. These men were professional mariners, either citizens or foreigners. The best helmsmen could command large salaries for their services. In contrast

to the oarsman the sailors shown here are dressed in caps and himation cloaks wrapped round their bodies: one is shown extending a hand to the oarsman as he boards, and the other is tending a cooking pot.

Both hoplites and archers might serve on a trireme as marines (*epibatai*). The number of marines was variable. At Lade in 494 each Chiot trireme had 40 picked men aboard (Hdt. 6. 15. 1) but this was an exceptionally large number. At Salamis each Athenian trireme had 10 marines and 4 archers aboard. Herodotus (7. 184. 2) assumes that the standard number of marines aboard ship would be 30.

Triremes could be used as horse- or troop-transports as well as fighting galleys. Horse-transports were rowed only by the upper row of 60 oarsmen and might carry 30 horses (Thuc. 6.43). The troop-carrier (*stratiotis*) had a more variable number of oarsmen and hoplite passengers up to the total of about 200 bodies which was allowed by the space of the trireme. So hoplites might also find themselves aboard ship as passengers on campaign.

The dolphin which the hoplite to the right uses as a shield device could be associated with the cults of Apollo Delphinios, who swam to Delphi in the form of a dolphin, Poseidon god of the sea, or Aphrodite Euploia, widely worshipped as goddess of the sea and seafaring. It has clearly been selected with reference to the dangers of his forthcoming voyage. His Corinthian helmet is worn on the crown of the head for comfort. He has decided not to fight with the protection of armour, hoping to swim to safety in case of disaster.

As well as the obvious dangers of the deep aboard ship, fire has been an age-old hazard in wooden ships. Triremes would hug the shore and the crew would disembark to cook their

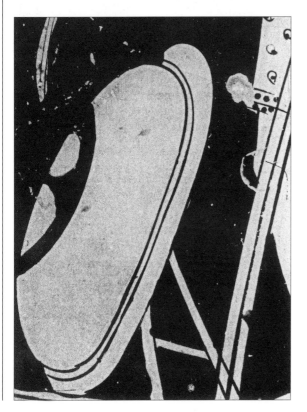

Aristophanes (*Acharn.* 1122, 1128–9) notes that when a shield had been taken down from the wall and out of its cover, it was steadied against a wooden trestle and polished with oil until all the tarnish had been removed and the shield was gleaming. A shield and such a trestle are shown on a pelike (inv. 1813) in the Palace of the Legion of Honour, San Francisco. (After *Corpus Vasorum Antiquorum*, USA 10 pl. 479, 1b)

LEFT **A young hoplite removes his shield from its cover. The shield's fig-leaf blazon was possibly connected with the cult of Apollo. Xenophon (*An.* 1.2.16) notes that the Ten Thousand carried their shields uncovered in a parade at Thymbara, suggesting that covers were also taken on campaign. From a cup (inv. 234) painted about 525 by the Bowdoin Eye-Cup Painter. (Staatliches Lindenau-Museum, Altenburg)**

RIGHT **The scene of a mobilised hoplite bidding farewell to his family is a staple of Greek vase art. He wears a *perizoma*. Note the Attic helmet with cheek-guards tied above the forehead and the apotropaic eye painted on the shield to let it 'see' incoming weapons. From a stamnos decorated by the Kleophon Painter around 440. (Staatliche Antikensammlungen, Munich, inv. 2415)**

meals. We see one cooking-pot (*chytra*) on a portable terracotta hearth, and a second one behind with a spout to let out steam if a lid was being used (the spout is hidden). The Greeks knew of no easy method of generating fire, therefore Greek armies would carry fire in cooking pots, even aboard ship.

E: THE STRATEGY OF DEVASTATION

An apron of thick material, probably called a *perizoma*, was sometimes worn wrapped around the waist beneath the groin-flaps of the cuirass to give extra protection against stabs with the spear which might otherwise make their way in between the flaps. In other cases a complete tunic of this thick material would be worn under the armour for comfort and extra protection. This tunic may have been called a *spolas*. Vase-paintings dating to after the Persian Wars show how hoplites started to discard their armour, but retained these light 'arming' garments to retain some form of protection.

1 wears a helmet of a type which has been called 'Thracian' on rather dubious grounds. It was suggested that the tall, domed skull evolved from the Thracian cap, but the Thracian cap was not, in fact, of this shape. The cheek-pieces of this

helmet are fully developed. Extending below the chin they give some defence to the throat, while the eyes and nose are shielded by a metal brim. The helmet type appears in Attic vase-painting from about 470 onwards, often in conjunction with the muscle-cuirass. This hoplite wears a tunic of thick material, however. His shield bears devices of the ball or ring, sun symbols sacred to Apollo, and crescent moons sacred to his sister Artemis. Below his shield he has attached a shield-apron decorated with an eye for extra protection, for he has also discarded his greaves.

The tunic worn under the armour could be very thin indeed. The Greek for tunic is *chiton*; modern authorities use the diminutive form *chitoniskos* for this light version. **2** wears a chitoniskos and an apron of thick material. His 'Illyrian' helmet, despite its name, probably evolved somewhere in the Peloponnese, where it enjoyed its greatest popularity. A huge number of examples were excavated in the Balkans in the late 19th century AD, hence the misleading name. Early Archaic examples were produced from two plates, riveted together over the crown, and overlapping so as not to present a vulnerable seam. As Greek bronze-smithing improved, the 'Illyrian' helmet was produced in one piece, but the two ridges on the crown survived as relics of its earlier construction. The 'Illyrian' helmet provided good vision and cover to the forehead and cheeks, but left the face exposed. It was not used in mainland Greece much into the 5th century BC.

Any citizens fit for work captured during these invasions would be sold as slaves. Those too old or too young for work would be killed: they could not be sold, and so otherwise would have to be fed in captivity. Death or slavery was also the frequent fate of the inhabitants of any city which was captured after a siege. Massacres of the enemy were common and whole nations could be extirpated by hoplite warfare.

F: HOPLITE DURING THE PELOPONNESIAN WAR

Hoplite equipment lightened further in the later 5th century BC. By the Peloponnesian War sometimes the only armour carried was a shield. **1** Our warrior has been given a blue tunic, but red, and especially crimson as the 'military' colour, was increasingly the standard colour preferred by hoplites.

He wears an *exomis*, a new type of tunic which replaced the *chitoniskos* towards the end of the 5th century BC. **2** It was made of two rectangles of material, usually linen, stitched most of the way up the sides to form a cylinder, leaving just enough space at the top for the arms to pass through. The two rectangles of material were only partially pinned or sewn together at the top, leaving an opening for the head. The wide cylinder of material was gathered up at the waist with a cloth belt tied in a reef knot, and fell down over the belt, hiding it from view, in a fold, or 'overfall'. **3** At either side of the opening left for the head, the top corners of the cloth rectangle would fall over the upper arms, sometimes giving the false impression that the tunic had short sleeves. **4** To allow freedom of movement to the right arm it was standard practice to undo the seam at the right shoulder and pass the right arm through the extended opening for the head. This allowed the tunic to hang loosely on the right side, forming a 'bag' of material under the right armpit.

Another garment worn by the hoplite was the shawl-like cloak, an elongated rectangle of material, known as an *ephaptis* or 'wrap'. **5** At the beginning of the 5th century BC it is shown wrapped around the waist like a loincloth. **6** By

The warrior, the basis for plate F, shown on this Attic grave stele from Megara, dating to about 420–410, squeezes a Lakonian pilos, clearly made of felt, in his right hand. He wears an *exomis* tunic with the seam let out over the whole of the right side. In his left hand he holds the butt of his spear, in a position suitable for the march, with the front handle of the shield held with the index finger. (Worcester Art Museum, Mass., inv. 1936.21)

BELOW **This example of a bronze *pilos*-helmet comes from Upper Egypt, where it had perhaps been lost or discarded by a Greek mercenary in Persian or Egyptian service. (Berlin, Staatliche Museen Inv. L. 41)**

This Gallo-Roman bronze statuette has probably become detached from a decorative piece of horse-furniture depicting a battle between gods and giants. This giant fights with a rock and his *ephaptis* cloak wrapped around his forearm. (Photo: István Rácz, Musée d'art et d'histoire, Geneva)

the end of the century it is normally draped over the elbows, as a type of shawl or light cloak. **7** In scenes depicting the hunt or a brawl, the ephaptis is often wrapped around the forearm for protection in a form of knot illustrated here.

In place of the close helmets worn earlier in the century hoplites, such as the one shown in the main figure, now wore only the felt caps previously worn underneath for comfort. Out of these felt caps grew new types of metal helmets which copied the caps in shape.

The 'Boeotian' helmet arose out of a wide-brimmed travelling hat. It was held in place by two straps, one under the chin, the other under the occipital bone at the back of the head. These straps were attached to a bronze fastener on either side of the hat. **8** In Greek art the hat is shown worn with the straps up, or with one or two of the straps down. **9** When both straps were down, the felt brim creased in two kinks either side of the ear. **10** The helmet which we call 'Boeotian' preserved this characteristic shape in bronze. The Greeks may have termed this type of helmet 'Boeotian' too. Xenophon (*On Horsemanship* 12.3) recommends the 'Boeotian-made' helmet as the type that best protects all parts above the cuirass without obstructing vision. The Boeotian helmet did, indeed, provide a good all-around view. **11** Another common type of travelling cap was the conical or 'sugar-loaf' shaped *pilos* cap. *Pilos* was the Greek word for felt. It was also sometimes worn under the helmet as a

'cap-comforter'. As hoplites discarded equipment in search of mobility, they adopted this cap instead of the helmet. **12** Eventually a new type of cap-helmet, which we know as the 'pilos-helmet', evolved, copying the shape of the felt cap in bronze. This type of helmet probably originated in Lakonia. During their defeat at Sphakteria in 425 the Lakedaimonians suffered greatly from the archery of their Athenian opponents. Thucydides (4.34.3) comments that they were poorly protected by their 'piloi', by which term he could mean either pilos-caps or helmets.

The cruciform sword (*xiphos*) remained popular during this period. **13** The iron blade and tang were forged in one piece. **14** The bronze or iron guard was normally made separately and slipped over the tang. **15** The hilt was also made separately, normally from wood or bone, but it could also be made of cast metal. It was hollow and fitted over the tang. **16** The cylindrical pommel, which could likewise be made of metal, wood or bone, was also fitted over the tang. **17** Finally a metal, normally bronze, finial was brazed onto the end of the tang to keep the hilt assembly in place.

The scabbard was made of two wooden laths (**18**), hollowed to receive the blade, glued together and held in place by a stitched leather cover, and by bone boxes which formed the mouth (**19**) and the chape (**20**) of the scabbard. The hilt of the sword was frequently accommodated within the mouth of the scabbard when

This sculpture of an Amazon shows how the sword (here a recurved sabre) was drawn from the scabbard with only one hand. The scabbard was normally suspended on a narrow cord under the armpit. Since the scabbard could not be gripped by the left (shield) hand, it was twisted up against the armpit, and the sword drawn downwards and out. (Athens, National Museum 3614, author's photo)

sheathed. **21** The baldric consisted of two lengths of cord passed over the right shoulder and tied in two sets of knots, forming a loop through which the sword and scabbard were passed resting under the left armpit.

G: LAKEDAIMONIAN BATTLE DRILL

The lightening of hoplite armour was accompanied, and possibly caused, by developments in tactics that required more speed on the battlefield. Above all it was the Lakedaimonians who perfected the tactical possibilities of hoplites.

The smallest unit employed in the Lakedaimonian battle line was the *enomotia*, or 'sworn band' of 36 men, which divided into three files of 12 men, each with a file-leader and file-closer. The file could be further divided into two half-files. The enomotia was commanded by an *enomotarches* who doubled as the file-leader of the right-hand file. The enomotarch would always occupy the front right position in the enomotia, the traditional Greek position of honour reserved for commanders. Xenophon (*Lak. Pol.* 11) states that the enomotia could be drawn up 'by one', 'by three' or 'by six'. In another passage (*Hell.* 6. 4. 12) he states that at

the battle of Leuktra the enomotia was drawn up 'by three' in files of 12. Presumably this was normal battle order.

There are problems interpreting Xenophon's information. This is especially true if we assume after Anderson that the frontage occupied by each hoplite was always two cubits, no matter how deep the phalanx may have been drawn up (a cubit measured one and a half feet). Fortunately Xenophon also left us another snippet of information in his *Cyropaedia* on how the 'ideal' phalanx changed formation. Thanks to Anderson we know that this was based on Lakedaimonian practice.

Xenophon's ideal enomotia deploys from single file to its 'by three' formation by the following simple mechanism. The second file-leader marches to the left of the file-closer of the first file and takes up a position to the left of the enomotarch. The third file-leader then marches to the left of the file-closer of the second file and takes up position to the left of the second file-leader.

The Spartan formation described by Xenophon was perhaps a precursor to the Macedonian formation, where each tactical unit occupied the same frontage however deep it was drawn up. According to this scheme the *enomotia* would always occupy a frontage of six cubits.

In loose order ('by one'), the enomotia was in single file and each soldier occupied a frontage of six cubits. This formation would have been ideal for marching rapidly into battle or over broken ground.

When drawn up 'by three', the enomotia was deployed in three files, and each soldier now occupied a frontage of two cubits. This corresponded to 'normal order' employed on the battlefield.

In the 'by six' formation half-leaders came forward between the files, giving the enomotia a frontage of six files. Each soldier now occupied just one cubit. Battlefield manoeuvres would have been practically impossible in this formation, which was presumably a 'super-dense order' adopted to receive a charge.

Four *enomotiai* made up a *lochos* or 'company'. In our reconstruction we see a lochos. The right-flank enomotia is drawn up 'by one' with the enomotarch at the front. To its left a second enomotia is moving from the 'by one' formation to 'by three', with the second file-leader marching forward to take up a position in front and to the left of the enomotarch. To its left a third enomotia has completed the formation change and is drawn up 'by three' with the file-leaders at the front. The fourth enomotia is drawn up 'by six'. For clarity the enomotarchs are distinguished by transverse crests, while file-leaders have fore-and-aft crests.

H: THE BATTLE OF KORONEIA, 394 BC

Desperate fights to the death, with massive casualties on both sides, were relatively rare in hoplite warfare. One exception was the battle of Koroneia. With the outbreak of the so-called Corinthian War, the Lakedaimonian King Agesilaos was recalled to Europe after his successful campaign against the Persians in Asia Minor. On his march back through Boeotia he was opposed by an army of Argives and Thebans. Xenophon (*Ages.* 2.9), an eyewitness of the battle, described the action in detail 'as there has been none like it in our time'.

Agesilaos was victorious on the right where the Argives fled before Agesilaos' army came into contact. The other allies on this flank fled 'when it came to spears' (Xen., *Hell.* 4.3.17). The Argives took refuge on nearby Mount Helicon. On the other flank the Theban phalanx broke through and reached the Lakedaimonian baggage train. Alerted of this, Agesilaos wheeled his phalanx around, prompting the Thebans to turn about in an attempt to reach the Argives on Mount Helicon. A desperate struggle ensued.

Xenophon (*Ages.* 2.14) describes the scene after the battle: 'Now that the battle was over, those gazing on could see where they had engaged one another, the ground stained crimson with blood, the corpses of friend and foe lying side by side, shields battered to pieces, spears snapped apart, swords naked of their scabbards, some lying in the dirt, some stuck in bodies, some still held in the hand'.

I: THE AFTERMATH OF BATTLE

This plate shows the aftermath of a hoplite battle. The victors are looking after their wounded, carrying off the dead and stripping the enemy corpses of armour, clothing and rings. In the background a trophy is being erected.

In the 360s the equipment of the hoplite changed dramatically in response to the new type of warfare first developed by the Theban general Epaminondas and then perfected by Philip and Alexander of Macedon. The muscle-cuirass dips at the abdomen to cover the groin, which must have made sitting or bending, as shown in this plate, extremely difficult. The monograms painted on the shields were the emblems of the Achaean and Arcadian Leagues.

This 4th-century BC Phrygian helmet was found at Vitsa in Epirus. Note the tubular crest-holders soldered onto the helmet at the sides of the temple and of the lobate crown. (Ioannina Museum 6419)

Achilles bandages Patroklos who has been wounded in the shield arm, probably by the arrow at bottom left which passed through his shield, and who wears a cap under his helmet. According to Herodotus (7.181) linen bandages and unguents were successfully used to treat battle wounds. Unusually Achilles wears sandals and a garter to prevent the chafing of the greaves, but no greaves themselves. From a kylix cup painted by the Sosias Painter around 500. (Ute Jung, Antikensammlung, Staatliche Museen zu Berlin – Preussischer Kulturbesitz, Berlin, F2278)

Gravestone of Athenian hoplite dating to about 340 found at Eleusis in AD 1888. Note the muscle-cuirass with shoulder-guards and three rows of pteruges, the ephaptis, the Phrygian helmet, the hoplite shield behind his legs and the lack of greaves. (Athens, National Museum 834)

J: HOPLITE, LATE 4TH CENTURY BC

1 The muscle-cuirass might have one, two, three or no rows of pteruges. **2** Normally both sides of the two plates were furnished with sets of hinges and rings. **3** The hinges (here viewed from the inside) on one side of the cuirass could be separated by removing the pins holding them together. The cuirass could now be opened out at this side, the hinges articulating at the other, put on, **4** and then closed together at the opened side with leather thongs tied round the two sets of rings. If the wearer was right-handed the pins would be removed and the cuirass would be tied on the right side and vice versa. Italian cuirasses are also supplied with a similar system of hinges and ties at the shoulders but

muscle-cuirasses from the Greek mainland are normally furnished with shoulder-pieces, often ornately decorated. **5** These shoulder-pieces were attached to the back-plate with a hinge and were secured in place on the breast-plate with a ring and tie system.

The 'Phrygian' helmet became common. It had no connection with Phrygia, but is so-named because its shape resembles the 'Phrygian bonnet' worn during Antiquity and copied during the French Revolution. It is similar in general form to the 'Thracian' helmet, except for the lobate end given to the domed skull. **6** The skull was normally made in one piece, and the cheek-pieces were plain, resembling those of a 'Chalcidian' helmet in outline. **7** Sometimes the cheek-pieces developed further on the shape of the 'Thracian' helmet, only leaving apertures for the eyes and mouth and frequently decorated with an embossed or incised moustache or beard. **8** The lobate skull must have been extremely difficult to construct, and examples have been found in Bulgaria with the skull constructed in three pieces and with the cheek-pieces decorated with an exuberant beard. These helmets probably equipped the guard of some local Thracian prince. **9** If plumes were worn with Phrygian helmets, they were generally fixed into bronze tubes soldered to the side of the skull.

By the Classical period spear-heads were made almost exclusively in iron. Classification is difficult. Many surviving examples are too corroded to be classified, and the fact that each weapon was forged individually contributes to a lack of uniformity in type. Whenever examples are recovered from sanctuaries or burials, there is always some uncertainty whether the spearhead was used in hunting or in warfare. A starting point is the system arrived at by Anthony Snodgrass, *Early Greek Armour and Weapons from the end of the Bronze Age to 600 b. c.* (1964). Many of the types identified there continued to be used into the Classical period.

10 Snodgrass Type E continues to be used into the 5th century BC. The socket is comparatively short, but the blade is long and wide with the midrib extending to the top. Some examples have small attachment holes at the bottom of the blade. **11** Type J, which appears in Classical contexts at the Isthmian Sanctuary, is likewise very long, but has a longer socket, a narrower blade, and sloping instead of rounded shoulders. Examples of this type can reach over half a metre in length. **12** Other examples of this type are shorter and with a wider blade. **13** Type R can be distinguished from Type J in not having a full-length midrib. The socket tapers to a point, overlapping the lower part of the blade, which is otherwise flat.

These long spear-head types are generally thought to belong to hoplite spears, but would perhaps be more suitable for hunting spears. The typical hoplite spear-head was small and leaf-shaped. **14** Type M is a small, plain type with a flat blade and a hammered tubular socket. It is the most popular type of spear-head dedicated at Isthmia during the Classical period. **15** This example, found in Corinth in a deposit of the middle or third quarter of the 4th century BC, is distinguished from Type M principally by its wide socket, widening towards the base, and equal in length to the leaf-shaped blade. The blade has a full length central midrib. **16** Some small spear-heads, like this example of Snodgrass Type F, continue to be made in bronze, even into the 5th century BC and perhaps beyond. **17** Type H can be even

Spear-heads came in a wide variety of shapes and sizes. These examples from Olympia, all of iron, are of (from the left) Snodgrass types M, P, M and J. (German Archaeological Institute, Athens, Neg. Ol. 2291)

BELOW **Early spear-butts end in a rectangular talon. This example from Olympia was, according to the inscription, dedicated as spoil taken by the Messenians from the Lakedaimonians, probably during the 460s. In the later 5th century BC the talon type of butt was replaced by a cylindrical tube, which flared in and out like a turned table leg.** (© German Archaeological Institute, Athens, Neg. No. Ol.2288)

smaller. Robinson identified this 4th century BC example from Olynthus as the head of a Macedonian pike (*sarisa*).

Spear-butts are even less well understood than the heads. **18** The characteristic shape at the beginning of the 5th century BC takes the shape of a talon, rectangular in section, attached to a socket. **19** In many examples the talon is separated from the socket by a ring. **20** Although the socket is normally plain, it might be decorated, usually with geometric incised ring pattern. All these examples are bronze, but iron was also used. **21** In many cases the shape of the bronze butts is copied and decorative bronze rings are added at the mouth of the socket and between the rectangular talon and circular socket. Other examples are simpler in shape. **22** This longer iron example has been fitted with a lead ring to correct the balance of the spear. **23** Some iron objects identified as spear-butts are, however, much smaller. **24** As the 5th century BC progresses and throughout the 4th century BC the butt gradually loses its rectangular talon, which becomes more rounded in shape, rather like the leg of a piece of furniture which has been turned on the lathe.

INDEX